THE WILD GAME INSTANT POT® COOKBOOK

THE WILD GAME INSTANT POT® COOKBOOK

Simple and Delicious Ways to Prepare Venison, Turkey, Pheasant, Duck, and Other Small Game

BY BEVERLY HUDSON

VOYAGEUR PRESS

© 2020 by Quarto Publishing Group USA Inc.

First published in 2020 by Voyageur Press, an imprint of The Quarto Group, 100 Cummings Center, Suite 265-D, Beverly, MA 01915, USA.
T (978) 282-9590 F (978) 283-2742 QuartoKnows.com

Voyageur Press titles are also available at discount for retail, wholesale, promotional, and bulk purchase. For details, contact the Special Sales Manager by email at specialsales@quarto.com or by mail at The Quarto Group, Attn: Special Sales Manager, 401 Second Avenue North, Suite 310, Minneapolis, MN 55401, USA.

10 9 8 7 6 5 4 3 2 1

ISBN: 978-0-7603-6924-1

Digital edition published in 2020
eISBN: 978-0-7603-6925-8

Library of Congress Cataloging-in-Publication Data is available.

Design and page layout: Tango Media Publishing Services, LLC
Food Styling: Natasha Taylor

Photo Credits
When multiple photos appear on a page, they are identified by letter, listed clockwise from the top left.
Cover and interior photographs by Glenn Scott, with the exception of pages 9, 10, 13, 15, 16, 28, 45, 54, 67, 84, 93, 98, 119, 122, 134, 141, 146, and 150.
Shutterstock.com: 9; 10; 13; 15; 16a, 16c, 16d, 16f; 28 (all); 54a, 54b, 54d, 54f; 84a, 84c, 84e, 84f; 98a, 98b, 98d, 98e, 98f; 122a, 122b, 122c, 122d, 122e; 134a, 134c, 134d, 134e, 134f; 148a, 148c, 148e, 148f; 150.

About the Author
Beverly Hudson is a writer and recipe developer. She lives in Minneapolis, Minnesota, with her husband and two cats.

The recipes in this book were originally developed by Teresa Marrone for the book *Slow Cookers Go Wild!*, which was published by Creative Publishing International in 2006.

Printed in China

CONTENTS

CHAPTER 6:
On the Side

CHAPTER 7:
Party Time

INTRODUCTION

Imagine coming inside after a cold day in the field—or a hard day at the office, for that matter—and being able to whip up a hearty, meltingly tender venison stew in minutes. With an Instant Pot, dishes that would otherwise take hours of simmering can be ready in no time. And with this book, you can prepare that stew, or any of these other tasty wild-game dishes, and have dinner on the table quickly and with very little last-minute work.

This book is written especially for hunters and for those who want to prepare wild game. Wild game is perfectly suited to pressure cooking, which excels at turning tough cuts of meat into tender morsels. If you have an Instant Pot, chances are good that you have plenty of recipes for beef, chicken, and pork—but how many do you have for venison, pheasant, and wild boar?

Wild game has different cooking characteristics than domestic meat, and for best results, you need to take this into account when preparing it, whether in an Instant Pot or slow cooker, on the stovetop or in the oven. Beef, for example, has much more external fat and internal marbling than venison; the meat is basted and tenderized as it cooks. Venison is quite lean, with virtually no internal marbling; the external fat tends to be strongly flavored and is removed during butchering. It follows, then, that a recipe for nicely marbled beef steaks won't work properly if prepared with lean venison steaks.

Domestic poultry is generally sent to market at a very young age, when the meat is still quite tender; plus, due to modern agricultural practices, chickens and domestic turkeys get very little exercise and

therefore do not develop muscle firmness. Compare that to a wild pheasant or wild turkey, which spends its life running in the fields and flying freely. Wild birds have to work hard to survive, and their meat is much less tender than that of domestic birds; plus, wild birds are often much older when harvested than are domestic birds (and meat from older animals is less tender than that from younger animals, whether domestic or wild).

Of course, wild game also tastes quite different than domestic meat. Wild turkeys and wild rabbits, for example, have meat that is darker and much more flavorful than that of their domestic cousins. Many wild boars are descendants of domestic pigs, but the similarity ends there; boar meat is richer and nuttier than domestic pork, with a much more aggressive flavor that most hunters find irresistible. Birds like ruffed grouse and Hungarian partridge have no domestic counterpart; and who ever heard of raising squirrels for meat?! All of these wild foods are unique and delicious, and they benefit from recipes that let their flavor shine through. The Instant Pot allows you to prepare wild game in a manner that retains all its natural flavor; most recipes are simple and quick to get started. What more could you ask for?

The Rise of the Modern Electric Pressure Cooker

The first pressure cooker was developed more than three hundred years ago by a French inventor who realized that trapping steam inside a pot as the liquid inside heated would increase the pressure on the liquid, meaning that more energy would be required to convert the liquid to gas and higher-than-boiling-point temperatures could be achieved for faster cooking. A pressure cooker designed for everyday home use was introduced in the United States in the 1930s.

It used to be the case that pressure cooking meant a giant, serious-looking stovetop contraption with a complicated lid, complete with dials and weighted valves and the nerve-wracking sense that the high-stakes situation could go south at any moment. The first electric pressure cookers came on the market in the 1990s and boasted mechanical timers and lids that automatically locked when the pot was under pressure—a welcome safety feature. But it wasn't until the Instant Pot brand began production of the digitally controlled electric pressure cooker, in 2010, that the super-high-heat cooking method really took off.

Now, instead of clamping down a heavy pot lid, adjusting the burner to achieve a high-pressure cooking environment, and carefully monitoring an analog pressure-gauge dial, all a home cook has to

do is twist on a lid (which will helpfully alert the user if it's not properly locked), push a couple of buttons, and wait for the appliance to signal with a charming bleep or two that its work is done. Cooking at high pressure has become easier and more convenient than ever: Not only is the process relatively straightforward, but the inner pot is easy to clean by hand or in the dishwasher, so there's no reason not to use the appliance often.

There are almost a dozen different models of Instant Pot (plus electric pressure cookers made by other brands) on the market now, in smaller- or larger-capacity sizes, with basic or more advanced capabilities. There are even models with Wi-Fi capability so you can control them from afar with your mobile device. Most models have features beyond pressure cooking that we won't need to use in this book but that are worth exploring—the yogurt-making, slow-cooker, rice-cooker, and sous vide functions, for example. In these wild game recipes, we focus exclusively on cooking at high pressure, and use the Sauté feature to brown meats and precook other ingredients before pressure cooking. The standard 6-quart (5.5 liter) size will work well for these dishes.

Step by Step Instant Pot Pressure Cooking

The process of pressure cooking with an Instant Pot varies a bit from model to model, and of course from recipe to recipe. Be sure to read through your Instant Pot's instruction manual before starting. For many of the dishes in this book, you'll follow these simple steps:

1. Brown the meat or vegetables. Turn the Instant Pot to Sauté, with the lid off. When it's reached the temperature you set (less/low, normal/medium, or more/high), the LED readout will indicate that the pot is hot. Don't worry about setting a time limit for sautéing—when you're done, you can just turn the appliance off by pushing Cancel. Add oil or another fat and the meat (or vegetables) and cook, stirring or turning occasionally with a long-handled wooden spoon or tongs, until the meat is nicely browned or prepared according to the recipe. You might have to do this in batches, removing meat to a bowl as it browns. Turn the Instant Pot off.

TIP: The lid of the Instant Pot features a wing on either side that fits neatly into a slot in the handle of the base to hold the lid vertically while sautéing or serving so you don't have to find a spot on the countertop for it.

2. Deglaze the pot. Pour in the liquid (wine, broth, or water, for example) and stir with a wooden spoon to scrape up all the browned bits on the bottom of the Instant Pot insert—clean it as well as you can. This is important for two reasons: First, the browned bits add lots of flavor to the dish. Second, cleaning the bottom of the pot of stuck-on food helps prevent the Instant Pot from overheating (it will indicate on the readout if it's overheating, and it will automatically turn off).

3. Add ingredients. Add the remaining ingredients that will be pressure cooked, including at least 1 cup (235 ml) total liquid so the Instant Pot can create enough steam to build pressure. Make sure you don't overfill the insert; for pressure cooking, the pot should not be more than two-thirds full. If your dish includes a large quantity of grains or dried beans, which will expand and create foam during cooking, don't fill the insert more than half full (and be sure to use plenty of liquid, of course).

4. Close the lid and seal the valve. With the Instant Pot still turned off, put the lid on and lock it in place securely, then turn the valve to Sealing for pressure cooking.

5. Set the pressure level and cooking time. This process varies among different models, so consult your instruction manual for details. See also the information about cooking at high altitudes on page 150.

On the basic Instant Pot models, you'll press the Manual button, then Pressure to select high pressure, then use the + and − signs to set the cooking time in minutes. The machine will beep to indicate that your settings have been accepted, and the pot will start to heat up. When the pressure inside has

reached a certain point—this could take anywhere from 5 to 30 minutes or so depending on how full the pot is—the minutes on the readout will begin to count down. You'll notice that the stainless-steel pin next to the sealing valve will be in the up position, with the top flush with the top of the lid, when the pot contents are at pressure. When the time is up, the Instant Pot will switch to Keep Warm. Turn off the Instant Pot by pressing Cancel.

6. Release the pressure. There are two ways to release the pressure, depending on the recipe instructions:

■ *Manual or quick pressure release* (generally used for lighter or more delicate meats and vegetable dishes): After turning off the Instant Pot, carefully, using tongs or an oven mitt to protect your hand from escaping steam, turn the valve to Venting and let the pressure dissipate. Again, take care to keep away from the flow of steam. When the steam has stopped spurting from the valve and the stainless-steel pin has dropped into the down position, you can unlock and remove the lid.

■ *Natural pressure release* (generally used for darker meats or larger roasts): After turning off the Instant Pot, simply let the pressure release on its own. There's no need to turn the vent; just wait until the stainless-steel pin has dropped into the down position, indicating that the pressure in the pot has dissipated, then unlock and remove the lid. Natural pressure release can take some time, but for larger roasts especially it keeps the meat from drying out and toughening. If you're in a hurry, you can let the pressure release naturally for 10 minutes or so, and then turn the valve to Venting to release it the rest of the way.

For many of the recipes here, that's it—the dish is ready to enjoy!

7. Thicken the sauce or cook off excess liquid, if necessary. Because the Instant Pot requires a certain amount of runny liquid in the pot to build up pressure, you'll sometimes be left with too much liquid at the end of the pressure-cooking time. You can either thicken the juices, as described under Using Thickeners below, or turn the Instant Pot to Sauté, with the lid off, and cook until some of the liquid has evaporated. If the meats or vegetables in the sauce are in danger of overcooking, spoon some of the liquid into a saucepan and boil it on the stovetop to reduce and thicken it before returning it to the pot.

8. Add the finishing touches. Some ingredients should only be added after pressure cooking, including fresh herbs or very delicate, quick-cooking vegetables like green peas; heavy cream, sour cream, or cheese; condensed soups or evaporated milk; and additional salt and pepper to taste.

TIP: Most Instant Pot models come with a wire rack or trivet that fits in the bottom of the pot insert. It's helpful for steaming vegetables above an inch or two of water, and for pressure cooking dishes like the Duck or Goose and Dressing (page 115) and the Instant Pot Dressing (page 132)—for those recipes, you'll also need a deep baking pan or casserole dish that fits in the Instant Pot on top of the rack.

Using Thickeners

Because thickening ingredients like flour and cornstarch can settle to the bottom of the insert and prevent the Instant Pot from building pressure properly, it's best to add these after the pressure-cooking time is up. The simplest way to thicken a sauce is to mix a slurry of all-purpose flour or cornstarch and cold water, stir it into the liquid in the pot, and simmer (using the Sauté feature if the liquid is not already at a simmer) until thickened. Use the following ratios as a guideline:

1 part all-purpose flour to 2 parts cold water
1 part cornstarch to 1 part cold water

You can also simply ladle some of the liquid from the pot into a small bowl, let it cool slightly, then stir in flour or cornstarch; return the liquid to the pot and simmer until thickened.

Mashing some of the soft-cooked vegetables or beans in the pot is another way to thicken the cooking liquids a bit.

Instant Pot Safety

Carefully read the instruction manual that came with your Instant Pot (the manuals are available to read online) before you use the appliance. A few important cautionary notes bear repeating:

■ Position your Instant Pot in a spot on your countertop with plenty of space around it—the metal outer housing will get hot. In addition, make sure there's free space above the pressure-release valve, where steam will come out (sometimes a great deal of it!) as pressure is released. The steam can loosen wallpaper and paint over time. Keep the cord tucked securely behind the Instant Pot to reduce the risk of snagging and pulling the appliance off the counter.

■ Dry off the outside of the stainless-steel insert before setting it into the Instant Pot, and perform regular cleanings of the outer pot, lid, valves, and condensation trap.

■ Never try to force the Instant Pot lid open before the pressure inside has fully dissipated and the stainless-steel pin valve has dropped into the down position.

■ Take special care with dried beans and grains, as they can foam up quite a bit under pressure and spurt foam out along with the steam if the manual (quick) pressure release method is used. Let the pressure release naturally instead.

■ Don't obstruct the pressure-release vent with your hand, a towel, or anything else.

Types of Game to Choose for the Instant Pot

If you took a survey asking people what foods are best for preparing in the Instant Pot, you'd consistently get two answers: beef stew and beef pot roast. That's because the moist heat provided by the pressure cooker is great for turning these less-tender cuts into melt-in-your-mouth delights. You might also hear that the Instant Pot does a good job on cut-up chicken, standard beef and pork roasts, chops, and casserole-type dishes.

Wild game is an even better candidate for pressure cooking. As noted above, it is less tender than similar domestic meats, so it benefits from moist cooking, like slow simmering, braising—and pressure cooking. Because of the difference in tenderness, wild game requires longer cooking times than domestic meat, so you'll want to keep that in mind if you're trying to prepare wild game using a recipe that was written for domestic meat. It's best to start with recipes that were developed especially for wild game; then, when you're comfortable preparing a few of those, you can try your hand at adapting some of your favorite domestic-meat recipes.

Venison is the perfect meat for preparing in the Instant Pot, using either the pressure-cooking function or the slow-cooking function. Note that *venison* refers not just to deer meat, but that from any of the hooved big-game animals, such as moose, elk, or antelope (all of which are interchangeable in recipes that call for venison). Because a deer or other

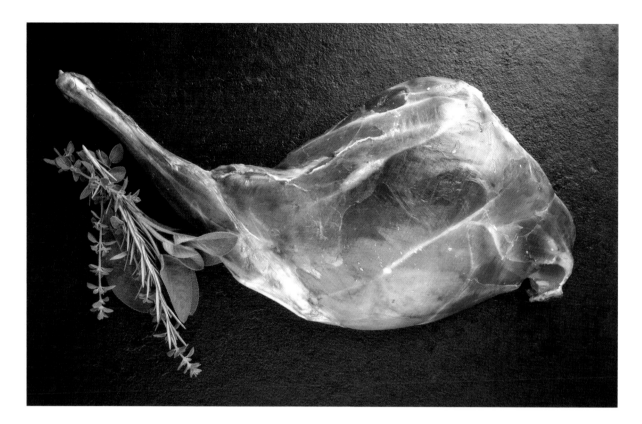

big-game animal yields so much meat, most hunters have an ample supply of it in the freezer. Plus, much of this meat falls into the less-than-tender category, making it ideal for pressure cooking. (Save your prime venison roasts, such as the tenderloin and backstrap, for dry-heat roasting in the oven or a countertop roaster, or on the grill.)

Ground venison can be prepared with the same recipes used for ground beef; the only difference—aside from the taste—is that ground venison may not have any fat added to it, so it will require oil when browning.

Squirrels and rabbits are a natural for the Instant Pot, but you won't find many recipes that you can easily adapt for them because they take so much longer to cook than, say, chicken parts. Cut-up upland gamebirds and waterfowl work well in the Instant Pot, and boneless, skinless gamebird meat works great in stews, casseroles, and other simmered dishes. The Instant Pot is not a good choice for preparing that whole prize turkey that you carefully plucked, nor for whole, skin-on pheasants or other gamebirds; the skin never browns and crisps as it does during oven-roasting, turning out wet and rubbery instead. Save those beautifully plucked, skin-on birds for the roaster or oven.

Approximate Cooking Times for Game Meats

Note that these are estimated times. Game is a wild product, and of course highly variable: Older animals, for example, may require longer cooking times than younger animals. If the meat isn't as tender or well-done as you'd like at the end of the time listed in the recipe, put the Instant Pot lid back on, set the valve to Sealing, and cook for another few minutes at high pressure.

TYPE OF GAME	APPROX. PRESSURE COOK TIME*	TYPE OF RELEASE
venison, boar, bear, moose		
ground	5 minutes	natural pressure release
venison/moose/elk roast	about 20 minutes/pound	natural pressure release
venison, large chunks	about 20 minutes/pound	natural pressure release
venison, small pieces	20 minutes	natural pressure release
boar roast	about 15 minutes/pound	natural pressure release
bear, large chunks	about 20 minutes/pound	natural pressure release
venison/boar ribs	20 minutes	natural pressure release
wild sheep		
small pieces	20 minutes	natural pressure release
rabbit		
pieces	15 minutes	natural pressure release
boneless	12 minutes	natural pressure release
squirrel		
pieces	15 minutes	natural pressure release
whole	20 minutes	natural pressure release
duck		
whole	20 minutes	quick pressure release
pieces	15 minutes	quick pressure release
breast	12 minutes	quick pressure release
boneless	12 minutes	quick pressure release
pheasant/grouse/partridge		
pieces	15 minutes	quick pressure release
drumsticks only	20 minutes	quick pressure release
boneless	12 minutes	quick pressure release
quail		
whole	8 minutes	quick pressure release
wild turkey		
pieces	20 minutes	quick pressure release
boneless	15 minutes	quick pressure release

*If you're using the Instant Pot Max, which cooks at higher pressure than the other models, be sure to read the instruction manual and adjust cooking times as necessary.

About the Recipes in This Book

All of the recipes in this book were written for electric pressure cookers like the Instant Pot.

When a recipe calls for a gamebird, or small game such as a rabbit or squirrel, it is assumed that the game has been properly field-dressed and has been plucked, skinned, or whatever is necessary to prepare it for the table. Skin should be removed from gamebirds and waterfowl (individual recipes will generally refer to this as well).

Feel free to substitute any type of hoofed big game for the venison that is called for in a recipe, as long as the cut is similar. For example, moose shoulder roast works just as well as deer shoulder roast in a pot roast, as long as the size is the same as what is called for in the recipe. Likewise, wild boar and javelina may be substituted for one another. Bear meat is rather in a class by itself, but if you have a freezer full of it, go ahead and try it in recipes that call for venison or wild boar; just make sure that bear, like wild boar and javelina, is always cooked to at least 165°F (74°C) due to concerns about trichinosis.

Most upland gamebirds can be freely substituted for another, as long as the size of the cut is similar; for example, you wouldn't want to substitute cut-up doves for cut-up pheasants, due to the size variation. But you could substitute Hungarian partridge pieces, or even chukar partridge pieces, for pheasant pieces. If a recipe calls for boneless, skinless meat from a specific upland gamebird, you may substitute an equal quantity of boneless, skinless meat from any other upland gamebird. Ducks and geese are interchangeable in the same way; boneless meat from one does fine as a stand-in for boneless meat from the other, and as long as the birds are fairly similar in size, you can substitute parts—for example, a cut-up snow goose can be used in place of a cut-up mallard.

Some vegetable prep is assumed and is not mentioned in the recipes. Onions and garlic are always peeled (unless specifically stated otherwise, as in Pheasant Braised with Whole Garlic on page 101); bell peppers are always stemmed and cored. Carrots and potatoes are generally peeled, but may be left unpeeled if you prefer; scrub them well before using. Turnips and other thick-skinned root vegetables are always peeled before further preparation. All fruits and vegetables should be well washed before cooking. By the way, a "rib" of celery is a single piece—not a whole bunch! When a recipe calls for vegetables to be diced, cut them into ¼-inch (6 mm) cubes or squares unless other measurements are given.

Aside from the game meats, these recipes call for ingredients that are easy to find in any decent supermarket, and those that are easy to store long-term at room temperature, like canned vegetables, dried beans, and spice blends. On page 148 you'll find a list of convenient pantry items you might wish to have on hand.

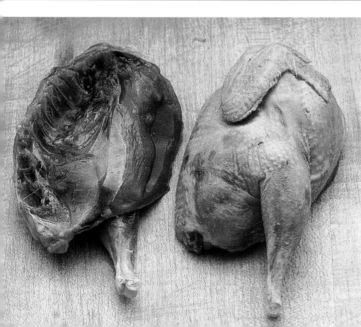

SANDWICHES AND SUCH

Wild Boar Burritos

Look for the dried ancho chile in a Mexican market, or with the specialty produce at a large supermarket.

4 TO 6 SERVINGS

Ingredients

1½-pound (680 g) wild boar roast

2 dried hot red peppers, or ¼ teaspoon hot red pepper flakes

1 dried ancho chile, optional

Half of an onion, cut into 1-inch (2.5 cm) chunks

2 or 3 cloves garlic, sliced

¼ cup (60 ml) beer or chicken broth

6 to 10 flour tortillas

Garnishes: Shredded cheese, prepared salsa, chopped onions, chopped tomatoes

Directions

Cut the boar into 1-inch (2.5 cm) chunks, discarding any tendons and excess fat. Place the boar in the Instant Pot. Break the peppers and chile, if using, into several pieces; add to the pot. Add the onion, garlic, beer, and ¾ cup (175 ml) water; stir well. Cover, turn the valve to Sealing, and cook on manual high pressure for 25 minutes. Turn off the Instant Pot and let the pressure release naturally. The meat should be very tender; if not, cook for another 5 minutes on high pressure.

Shred the meat coarsely with two forks. Turn the Instant Pot to Sauté on more/high heat and cook for about 10 minutes longer, until it reaches the desired consistency.

Heat the tortillas briefly in a microwave or oven. Serve the meat with tortillas and garnishes.

Sloppy Does

You'll love this quick and easy twist on classic Sloppy Joes, which uses ground venison in place of beef.

Ingredients

2 teaspoons vegetable oil

1½ pounds (680 g) ground venison

1 medium onion, chopped

Half of a green or red bell pepper, chopped

1 rib celery, chopped

2 cloves garlic, chopped

¾ cup (180 ml) ketchup

¾ cup (175 ml) beef broth

2 tablespoons packed brown sugar

2 tablespoons prepared mustard

2 tablespoons vinegar

1 tablespoon Worcestershire sauce

1 teaspoon seasoned salt

¼ teaspoon ground cayenne pepper, optional

6 to 8 hamburger buns

Directions

Set the Instant Pot to Sauté on more/high heat and let it heat up. Add the oil and venison and cook until the venison is no longer pink, stirring frequently to break up the meat. Add the onion, bell pepper, celery, and garlic; cook, stirring occasionally, until the vegetables are tender-crisp, about 5 minutes. Pour off the excess grease. Add the remaining ingredients except the buns; stir well. Turn off the Instant Pot. Cover, turn the valve to Sealing, and cook on manual high pressure for 5 minutes. Turn off the Instant Pot and let the pressure release naturally. If the mixture is too liquid, set the Instant Pot to Sauté on more/high heat and cook until it reaches the desired consistency. Spoon the meat mixture into the split buns.

Italian Garlic Hoagies

Try warming the rolls before serving to make these hoagies even more of a crowd pleaser.

Ingredients

4-pound (1.8 kg) venison roast

5 cloves garlic

1 teaspoon dried marjoram leaves

1 teaspoon dried thyme leaves

½ teaspoon hot red pepper flakes

2 teaspoons olive oil

2 cups (475 ml) beef broth

1 packet (1 to 1¼ ounces/ 32 to 40 g) dry onion soup mix

3 bell peppers, sliced

6 to 8 hoagie rolls

Directions

Pat the venison roast dry with paper towels. In a mini food processor, combine the garlic, marjoram, thyme, pepper flakes, and olive oil; process the mixture until very fine (alternatively, you can press the garlic through a garlic press or chop finely by hand, then combine it in a small bowl with the herbs, hot pepper, and oil). Rub the garlic mixture all over the roast. Add the broth and 1 cup (235 ml) water to the Instant Pot. Place the roast in the Instant Pot; sprinkle with the onion soup mix. Cover, turn the valve to Sealing, and cook on manual high pressure for 80 minutes. Turn off the Instant Pot and let the pressure release naturally.

Remove the roast from the Instant Pot; turn the Instant Pot to Sauté on more/high heat. Slice or shred the roast and return the meat to the Instant Pot. Add the bell pepper strips and stir well; cook until the peppers are just tender. Serve the meat and peppers on split hoagie rolls, with desired accompaniments.

REMOVING SILVERSKIN FROM GAME

Silverskin is a thin but tough membrane that separates muscle groups in big game. It looks like a shiny, silvery layer on the outside of the meat. It is tough and can cause uneven cooking, so it should be removed.

A very sharp fish-fillet knife is the best tool to remove silverskin; the long, flexible blade allows you to remove the silverskin without cutting away too much meat. Removing silverskin is much like skinning a fish fillet; the knife should slip between the silverskin and the meat while your fingertips apply pressure to the silverskin, holding it in place.

Place the meat on a cutting board, with the silverskin facing down. Cut down into one end of the meat just to the silverskin, then grab the silverskin with your fingernails. Turn the knife blade sideways and scrape toward the other end of the meat, keeping the knife at a slight downward angle. Continue cutting the silverskin off in strips until the meat is clean. With a little practice, you'll be able to remove the silverskin in long strips with virtually no meat attached.

Venison Cheese Steak Sandwiches

Creamy coleslaw, baked beans, and corn on the cob are perfect accompaniments to these tasty sandwiches.

6 SERVINGS

Ingredients

1½ pounds (680 g) boneless venison steak, well trimmed before weighing

Garlic pepper, seasoned pepper, or coarsely ground black pepper

¼ teaspoon salt

2 tablespoons Worcestershire sauce

½ can (10½-ounces/298 g) condensed golden mushroom soup

⅓ cup (42 g) shredded Parmesan cheese

1 small onion, cut into thin rings

1 green or red bell pepper (or a mix of colors), halved from top to bottom and sliced into half rings

6 hoagie rolls, split and toasted

6 slices (1 ounce/28 g each) Swiss or Muenster cheese

Garnishes: Shredded lettuce, sliced tomatoes, thinly sliced onions, sliced bread-and-butter pickles, mayonnaise, pickled hot peppers

Directions

Cut the venison into ½-inch-wide (1.25 cm) strips. Put the strips into the Instant Pot with the garlic pepper, salt, Worcestershire sauce, and ¾ cup (175 ml) water. Cover, turn the valve to Sealing, and cook on manual high pressure for 20 minutes. Turn off the Instant Pot and let the pressure release naturally.

Turn the Instant Pot to Sauté on more/high heat. Add the condensed soup, Parmesan cheese, onion, and bell pepper; stir gently to mix. Cook until the onion and pepper are tender and the excess liquid has cooked off. Serve the steak strips and sauce in rolls with sliced cheese and any garnishes you like; for a nicer presentation, fill split rolls with venison mixture, top with cheese slices (cut in half to cover the meat), and broil until the cheese melts.

Variation: Golden Venison-Mushroom Casserole

Follow the recipe above, using a full can of condensed soup. Eliminate the hoagie rolls, cheese, and garnishes. Cook the mixture as directed; serve over hot cooked noodles or rice.

Blue-Plate Special: Open-Faced Turkey Sandwiches

Bone-in pieces add flavor to dishes like this, but the bones can fall out of the cooked meat into the gravy. If you use bone-in pieces, pick through the gravy very well with a slotted spoon and pull out any bones that have slipped out; also caution diners to watch for stray bones!

5 OR 6 SERVINGS

Ingredients

2 tablespoons butter or margarine

6 to 8 ounces (175 to 225 g) fresh mushrooms, sliced

2 pounds (900 g) boneless, skinless wild turkey pieces (breast halves and/or thighs), or 2½ pounds (1.1 kg) bone-in, skinless pieces

Poultry seasoning or other seasoning blend

¼ cup (35 g) all-purpose flour, or more if needed

2 envelopes (generally about 1 ounce/28 g each, depending on brand) turkey gravy mix*

For serving: Hot buttered toast, prepared mashed potatoes, cranberry sauce

Directions

Turn the Instant Pot to Sauté on normal/medium heat and let it heat up. Add the butter and mushrooms to the Instant Pot and sauté until just tender. Stir in 1 cup (235 ml) water.

Season turkey to taste with the seasoning of your choice. Place the turkey pieces in the Instant Pot. Cover, set the valve to Sealing, and cook on manual high pressure for 20 minutes. Turn off the Instant Pot and carefully turn the valve to Venting to release pressure.

With a slotted spoon, transfer the turkey pieces to a cutting board and set aside to cool slightly. Use a slotted spoon to pick through the gravy in the Instant Pot to remove any bones, if necessary (see note above).

In a large measuring cup or medium bowl, stir the flour and the envelopes of gravy mix into 1½ cups (355 ml) water. Stir mixture into the liquid in the Instant Pot; turn the Instant Pot to Sauté on normal/medium heat and cook until the gravy thickens, 15 to 30 minutes. If the gravy is too thin, stir together 2 tablespoons more flour and ¼ cup (60 ml) water and stir mixture into gravy; cook until desired thickness.

Meanwhile, remove the turkey meat from the bones if necessary; discard the bones and any tendons. Using two forks, break the meat into large shreds or chunks; return the meat to the gravy in the Instant Pot and stir gently.

Prepare the mashed potatoes and toast. For each serving, arrange toast on the edges of a plate. Scoop some mashed potatoes, turkey, and gravy into the middle of the plate; place a generous spoonful of cranberry sauce alongside.

★If you like, use one envelope of turkey gravy mix and one envelope of mushroom gravy mix.

Moose Au Jus (French Dip)

A few pantry items form the base of this hearty dipping sauce.
Choose a roast from the hindquarters, such as a rump or round portion,
rather than a front-quarter roast. The hindquarter roasts have
a finer texture and will slice more cleanly.

6 TO 8 SERVINGS

Ingredients

2- to 2½-pound (1 to 1.1 kg)
moose, elk, or venison roast
(see note above)

Garlic salt, coarsely ground
black pepper, and dried
herb blend

1 can (10½ ounces/298 g)
condensed beef broth

½ cup (120 ml) red wine

2 tablespoons soy sauce

1 large onion, thinly sliced

Crusty French-bread-style rolls,
or crusty baguettes

Directions

Remove any silverskin and fat from the roast (see sidebar on page 22); pat dry with paper towels. Sprinkle the roast generously with salt, pepper, and herbs; rub the seasoning into the meat.

In the Instant Pot, stir together the broth, wine, soy sauce, and ½ cup (120 ml) water. Scatter the sliced onions over the bottom of the Instant Pot. Place the roast on the onions. Cover, turn the valve to Sealing, and cook on manual high pressure for 40 minutes. Turn off the Instant Pot and let the pressure release naturally.

Transfer the roast to a cutting board; let it stand for about 10 minutes. Turn the Instant Pot to Sauté on less/low heat to keep the juices warm.

Split the rolls or baguettes most of the way through, leaving one side connected like a hinge; if you are serving baguettes, cut them into individual portions. Scoop out a bit of bread from the center of each roll to create a space for the meat.

Slice the roast thinly across the grain. Return the sliced meat to the Instant Pot; stir gently to combine the meat with juices. Fill the rolls with the meat slices and onions; serve juices from the Instant Pot in bowls for dipping.

CHAPTER 2

SOUPS AND CHILI

Pheasant and Noodle Soup

Feel free to substitute grouse, partridge, or wild turkey for the pheasant; you will need about 2 pounds (1 kg) of bone-in pieces. If using wild turkey, increase the pressure-cooking time to 20 minutes.

6 SERVINGS

Ingredients

1 pheasant, skin and any fat removed, cut into serving pieces

2 carrots, sliced

2 ribs celery, sliced

Half of a small onion, diced

2 tablespoons minced fresh parsley

6 cups (1.4 liters) chicken broth

1 bay leaf

2 cups (90 g) uncooked curly egg noodles

½ teaspoon dried oregano leaves

½ teaspoon dried marjoram leaves

Salt and pepper

Directions

In the Instant Pot, combine the pheasant, carrots, celery, onion, parsley, broth, and bay leaf. Cover, set the valve to Sealing, and cook on manual high pressure for 15 minutes. Turn off the Instant Pot and carefully turn the valve to Venting to release the pressure.

With a slotted spoon, transfer the pheasant to a cutting board and set it aside to cool slightly; remove and discard the bay leaf. Use a slotted spoon to pick through the soup mixture to remove any bones. Set the Instant Pot to Sauté on more/high heat and add 2 cups (475 ml) water. When boiling, add the noodles, oregano, and marjoram; cook until the noodles are tender.

Meanwhile, remove the pheasant meat from the bones; discard the bones and any tendons. Cut the pheasant into bite-size pieces and return it to the Instant Pot. Taste for seasoning and add salt and pepper as necessary. Caution your diners to watch for stray bones that may have escaped your notice.

Mexican Pheasant Chowder

This creamy soup is great topped with crushed tortilla chips or popcorn. A sprinkling of crumbled queso fresco (fresh Mexican cheese) is a nice touch also.

6 SERVINGS

Ingredients

1 quart (1 liter) chicken broth or pheasant stock (page 52)

¾ pound (340 g) boneless, skinless pheasant meat, cut into bite-size pieces

1 cup (120 g) frozen whole-kernel corn, thawed

1 can (15 ounces/425 g) whole potatoes, drained and diced

1 jar (2 ounces/57 g) diced pimientos, drained

1 envelope (1.25 ounces/35 g) taco seasoning mix

1 cup (227 g) sour cream (reduced-fat works fine)

1 can (10½ ounces/305 g) condensed cream of potato soup

1 cup (235 ml) nacho cheese dip*

3 tablespoons (45 ml) minced fresh cilantro, optional

Directions

In the Instant Pot, combine the broth, pheasant, corn, potatoes, pimientos, and taco seasoning. Cover, set the valve to Sealing, and cook on manual high pressure for 12 minutes. Turn off the Instant Pot and carefully turn the valve to Venting to release the pressure.

Ladle about 1 cup (235 ml) of the hot soup into a mixing bowl; stir in the sour cream and condensed soup, mixing well. Add the sour cream mixture, cheese dip, and cilantro, if using, to the Instant Pot; let the mixture stand for 5 minutes to heat through. (If necessary, turn the Instant Pot to Sauté on normal/medium heat to heat through.)

If you have leftovers, reheat them gently but do not boil; the soup could curdle if it is overheated.

*Nacho cheese dip is a cheesy sauce that can be found with the snack chips at the supermarket. You could substitute half an 8-ounce (225 g) package of pasteurized-process cheese (plain or with jalapeños), cut into cubes.

Scotch Broth with Wild Sheep

Wild sheep is particularly appropriate for this update on a traditional shepherd's dish, but you can substitute any other big-game meat, such as venison, antelope, or bear, for the sheep. I like to grind fresh black pepper over my portion; fresh chopped parsley is also a nice garnish.

---

5 TO 7 SERVINGS

Ingredients

12 ounces (340 g) boneless wild sheep or other big game (see note above), well trimmed before weighing

1 quart (1 liter) beef broth

¾ cup (145 g) pearled barley (not instant barley), rinsed

3 medium carrots, diced

2 small ribs celery, diced

1 medium turnip, diced

1 medium onion, diced

1 teaspoon salt

½ teaspoon dried thyme

¼ teaspoon coarsely ground black pepper

1 bay leaf

Directions

Cut the meat into bite-size pieces. Place the meat in the Instant Pot with all the remaining ingredients and 2 cups (475 ml) water. Cover, set the valve to Sealing, and cook on manual high pressure for 20 minutes. Turn off the Instant Pot and let the pressure release naturally. Remove the bay leaf before serving. If the soup is too thick, thin with a little hot water.

REDUCING THE FAT

Condensed creamy soups are great for adding richness to stews and casseroles, but they are fairly high in fat. Campbell's has a line of reduced-fat condensed creamy soups, and these work just great in these dishes.

I also use evaporated nonfat milk in much of my cooking, to replace cream or half-and-half in recipes (don't try this for baking, though). A half cup (120 ml) of heavy cream has 5.5 grams of fat; light cream has 2.9 grams of fat. The same amount of evaporated nonfat milk has 0.3 gram of fat, and it works great in soups and casseroles.

Sour cream is available in light and nonfat varieties. I personally find the nonfat stuff to be chalky and prefer not to use it, but the light sour cream works fine in soups, casseroles, and sauces. As always, add sour cream at the end, after the pressure-cooking step is complete.

Thai Pheasant Soup

This recipe uses a few Thai staples that can be found in most large supermarkets or at a specialty Asian grocer. Be sure to buy unsweetened coconut milk, not the thicker, sweetened coconut cream that is used for tropical drinks. The rice sticks used here are shaped like thin spaghetti with a rough texture; they are sometimes called mai fun. *You can substitute any type of rice sticks you like; Asian markets offer a variety of options.*

5 OR 6 SERVINGS

Ingredients

Boneless, skinless breast meat from 1 pheasant

2 small fresh hot red peppers, stems and seeds removed

1 strip lemon zest (yellow part only), 1 x 2 inches (2.5 x 5 cm)

3 slices peeled fresh gingerroot, each about ¼ inch (6 mm) thick

1 clove garlic

1 quart (1 liter) chicken broth or pheasant broth (page 52), divided

1 can (7 ounces/199 g) sliced mushrooms, drained

2 tablespoons Thai fish sauce (nam pla)*

2 tablespoons packed brown sugar

2 to 3 ounces (60 to 90 g) thin rice sticks (see note above)

1 can (14 ounces/414 ml) reduced-fat unsweetened coconut milk (see note above)

6 green onions, sliced (white and green parts)

¼ cup (4 g) whole fresh cilantro leaves (loosely packed, stems removed)

1 lime, cut into wedges

Directions

Cut the pheasant breast into strips that are about ¼ x ¼ x 2 inches (6 mm x 6 mm x 5 cm); add them to the Instant Pot. Slice the hot peppers into very thin strips; add them to the Instant Pot.

In a blender, combine the lemon zest, gingerroot, garlic, and about 1 cup (235 ml) of the broth; blend until smooth, then pour the mixture into the Instant Pot. Add the remaining broth, mushrooms, fish sauce, and brown sugar to the Instant Pot. Cover, set the valve to Sealing, and cook on manual high pressure for 12 minutes. Turn off the Instant Pot and carefully turn the valve to Venting to release the pressure.

Heat a saucepan of water to boiling. Break the rice sticks into shorter lengths if you like (this makes them easier to eat), then add them to the boiling water and cook until just done, 4 to 5 minutes. They will still be somewhat chewy. Drain the noodles and add them to the Instant Pot, along with the coconut milk, green onions, and cilantro leaves. Set the Instant Pot to Sauté on normal/medium heat and cook for 15 minutes longer. Serve with the lime wedges so each person can squeeze some lime juice into their soup.

*If fish sauce is unavailable, substitute light soy sauce; for a more authentic flavor, also add a pinch of mashed anchovy.

Duck and Sausage Gumbo

Gumbo is a traditional Southern dish that is somewhere between a soup and a stew. The roux—a mixture of flour and oil that is slowly cooked until deep brown—is an essential part of the dish, as is the okra; both help thicken the gumbo and provide the traditional taste. If you don't have venison sausage, substitute any smoked sausage links.

8 SERVINGS

Ingredients

½ cup (125 ml) vegetable oil

½ cup (70 g) all-purpose flour

2 medium onions, diced

3 ribs celery, diced

2 green bell peppers, diced

3 cloves garlic, minced

Boneless, skinless meat from 2 wild ducks, cut into bite-size pieces

1 pound (455 g) smoked, fully cooked venison sausage links, sliced

1 quart (1 liter) chicken broth

2 cans (14½ ounces/411 g each) diced tomatoes, undrained

1 tablespoon Worcestershire sauce

1 teaspoon pepper, preferably freshly ground

1 package (9 ounces/255 g) frozen sliced okra, thawed

½ teaspoon dried oregano leaves

Hot cooked rice

Tabasco or another liquid hot sauce, optional

Directions

Set the Instant Pot to Sauté on normal/medium heat. Add the oil. With a whisk, blend in the flour. Cook, stirring constantly with a whisk (or a wooden spoon, once the roux has cooked for a few minutes), until the mixture is a deep golden brown and has a nutty smell; this will take 10 to 15 minutes.

Add the onions, celery, bell peppers, and garlic to the Instant Pot; cook, stirring constantly, for about 5 minutes. Then add the duck, sausage links, broth, tomatoes, Worcestershire sauce, and ground pepper and stir well to lift any browned bits and roux from the bottom of the pot and incorporate them into the mixture. Turn off the Instant Pot. Cover, set the valve to Sealing, and cook on manual high pressure for 12 minutes. Turn off the Instant Pot and carefully turn the valve to Venting to release the pressure. Add the okra and oregano. Set the Instant Pot to Sauté on more/high heat and cook until the okra is tender. Serve the gumbo in soup plates, atop a scoop of hot white rice. Many people enjoy Tabasco or another liquid hot sauce with gumbo.

Variation: Goose and Sausage Gumbo

Substitute 1 pound (455 g) boneless, skinless goose meat for the duck. Proceed as directed.

Lentil and Upland Gamebird Soup

Unlike most dry beans, lentils don't require pre-soaking prior to cooking. This is a good recipe to use with shot-up birds; be sure to pick out all shot and bone fragments before putting the meat into the Instant Pot.

6 TO 8 SERVINGS

Ingredients

1 pound (455 g) boneless, skinless pheasant or other upland gamebird meat

¾ pound (about 2⅔ cups/ 340 g) dry lentils, rinsed and picked over

2 carrots, sliced ¼ inch (6 mm) thick

2 ribs celery, diced

1 small onion, diced

1 quart (1 liter) chicken broth

1 medium tomato, diced

2 tablespoons freshly squeezed lemon juice

½ teaspoon ground turmeric, optional (adds nice color)

½ teaspoon crumbled dried rosemary leaves

2 bay leaves

A pinch of sugar

Leaves from several sprigs fresh parsley, chopped

Directions

Cut the pheasant into bite-size pieces, being careful to remove any shot or bone. Add to the Instant Pot with 2 cups (475 ml) water and all the remaining ingredients except the parsley. Cover, set the valve to Sealing, and cook on manual high pressure for 12 minutes. Turn off the Instant Pot and carefully turn the valve to Venting to release the pressure. Remove and discard the bay leaves. Stir well; sprinkle with the parsley and add salt if necessary just before serving. If the soup is thicker than you like, simply add some more hot water or stock to thin it to the desired consistency.

Steak and Barley Soup

Venison from the shoulder, shanks, or rump works well in this hearty soup. Be sure to remove any silverskin (see page 22) or tendons before weighing the meat.

=== **4 SERVINGS** ===

Ingredients

1 pound (455 g) boneless venison roast or stew pieces (see note above, and sidebar below)

Salt and pepper

2 tablespoons vegetable oil

1 quart (1 liter) beef broth

2 medium carrots, diced

1 rib celery, diced

1 small onion, diced

1 can (14½ ounces/411 g) diced tomatoes, undrained

¾ cup (175 ml/145 g) pearled barley (not instant barley), rinsed

1 tablespoon soy sauce

Directions

Pat the venison dry; cut it into strips that are about ¼ x ½ x 1½ inches (6 mm x 1.25 cm x 3.75 cm). Season with salt and pepper to taste. Set the Instant Pot to Sauté on normal/medium heat; add the oil and the venison and brown on both sides. Add the broth and scrape up any browned bits, then add the remaining ingredients; stir to blend. Cover, set the valve to Sealing, and cook on manual high pressure for 20 minutes. Turn off the Instant Pot and let the pressure release naturally.

GETTING THE MOST FROM VENISON

If you butcher your own deer, you'll end up with lots of scraps. I like to keep two separate bowls for scraps as I go: one for scraps from less-tender areas such as the shoulder, and another for choice scraps from the backstrap or round. As soon as I've got a pound (455 g) or so of scraps in one of the bowls, I pack it into a labeled freezer-weight zipper bag and pop it into the freezer; later, I wrap the frozen package in freezer paper.

The less-tender scraps are great for turning into sausage or using in stews, while the choice scraps work well for recipes such as stroganoff, stir-fries, and other dishes. For the Steak and Barley Soup, choose stew scraps; the Instant Pot will make them deliciously tender.

Turkey and Wild Rice Soup

This delicious and hearty soup takes a quick bit of last-minute prep shortly before serving; other than that, it couldn't be any easier.

6 TO 8 SERVINGS

Ingredients

¾ to 1 pound (340 to 455 g) boneless, skinless turkey meat, cut into bite-size pieces

½ cup (90 g) uncooked wild rice, rinsed and drained

1 quart (1 liter) chicken broth

2 or 3 carrots, sliced

1 russet potato (peeled or unpeeled, as you prefer), diced

1 rib celery, sliced

Half of a small onion, chopped

1 can (10½ ounces/305 g) condensed cream of mushroom soup (reduced-fat works fine)

1 can (12 ounces/354 ml) evaporated fat-free milk, or 1½ cups (350 ml) half-and-half

1 teaspoon dried herb blend

Salt and pepper

Directions

In the Instant Pot, combine the turkey, wild rice, and broth. Cover, set the valve to Sealing, and cook on manual high pressure for 15 minutes. Turn off the Instant Pot and carefully turn the valve to Venting to release the pressure.

Add the carrots, potato, celery, and onion. Cover, set the valve to Sealing, and cook on manual high pressure for another 5 minutes. Turn off the Instant Pot and carefully turn the valve to Venting to release the pressure.

Add the condensed soup, evaporated milk, and herb blend to the soup; season to taste with salt and pepper. Set the Instant Pot to Sauté on more/high heat and cook until the soup is hot but not boiling.

ABOUT WILD RICE

True wild rice is a precious commodity that is quite different from the paddy-grown "wild" rice that is sold in most stores. Paddy rice is a hybrid of the original wild grain; it has been manipulated to make growing and harvest easier and to produce a more uniform product. However, connoisseurs appreciate the flavor and integrity of true, hand-harvested wild rice, which is lighter in color and has a nuttier flavor than the commercial variety. True wild rice often has thicker grains and may show a good deal of color variation within the batch. Paddy-grown rice is often artificially darkened by smoking, and the grains may be thinner and longer than genuine wild rice.

To obtain true wild rice, search out a Native American community in a wild-rice area (Minnesota and Wisconsin are prime areas), or look for a label that states that the rice is wild-grown and hand-harvested. I think you will be amazed at the flavor difference of the true wild variety; it's definitely worth seeking out. For mail order, try the White Earth Land Recovery Project at www.nativeharvest.com. You may also be able to find a local wild-foods harvester who sells hand-harvested wild rice.

Bear Borscht

There are many ways to make borscht. Some variations use beets, while others use cabbage instead. This one features both, and substitutes rich, hearty bear meat in place of the beef short ribs that are usually used; you could substitute venison for the bear. Serve with thick slices of dark pumpernickel bread.

6 TO 8 SERVINGS

Ingredients

2 tablespoons butter

1 large onion, coarsely chopped

Half of a small head of green cabbage, cored and thinly sliced crosswise

2 cloves garlic, minced

1½ pounds (675 g) boneless bear roast or steaks, well trimmed before weighing

2 medium tomatoes, peeled, cored, seeded (see sidebar on page 47), and cut into large chunks

6 cups (1.4 liters) beef broth

3 tablespoons rice vinegar

1 tablespoon sugar

2 teaspoons salt

2 medium carrots, coarsely chopped

1 large russet potato, peeled and cut into ⅜-inch (1 cm) dice

2 medium beets (uncooked), peeled and cut into ¼-inch (6 mm) dice

Sour cream for garnish

Directions

Set the Instant Pot to Sauté on normal/medium heat and let it heat up. Add the butter and melt. Add the onion; cook for about 5 minutes, stirring occasionally. Add the cabbage and garlic; cook for about 10 minutes longer, stirring occasionally, then turn off the Instant Pot. Scrape all the contents of the pot into a bowl and set aside.

Cut the bear meat into 3 or 4 large chunks and add them to the Instant Pot, along with the tomatoes, broth, vinegar, sugar, and salt. Cover, set the valve to Sealing, and cook on manual high pressure for 30 minutes. Turn off the Instant Pot and let the pressure release naturally.

Pull the meat out of Instant Pot, shred it with two forks, and return the shreds to the soup, along with the sautéed vegetables, carrots, potato, and beets. Cover, turn the valve to Sealing, and cook on manual high pressure for 5 minutes. Turn off the Instant Pot and let the pressure release naturally. Serve the soup in wide soup plates with a dollop of sour cream on each serving.

Taco Soup

This is a thick, hearty soup that is almost chili-like. If you like a bit of spice, use Mexican-style stewed tomatoes (with jalapeño) and both envelopes of taco seasoning mix.

6 TO 8 SERVINGS

Ingredients

1 teaspoon vegetable oil

1 pound (455 g) ground venison

1 can (14½ ounces/411g) stewed tomatoes, undrained

3 cups (690 ml) beef or chicken broth

1 medium yellow onion, diced

1 green bell pepper, diced

1 can (15 ounces/425g) pinto beans, drained and rinsed

1 can (15 ounces/425g) black beans with cumin, undrained

1 can (8 ounces/227g) tomato sauce

1 or 2 envelopes (1.25 ounces/ 35g each) taco seasoning mix

3 tablespoons cornmeal

Garnishes: Diced avocado, shredded Monterey Jack cheese, sour cream, corn chips

Directions

Set the Instant Pot to Sauté on normal/medium heat. Add the oil and venison and cook until the venison is no longer pink, stirring to break it up. Turn off the Instant Pot. Drain off and discard any excess grease.

Add the tomatoes with their juices; break up any large tomato pieces with a spatula or your hands. Add the broth, onion, bell pepper, beans, tomato sauce, and taco seasoning. Cover, set the valve to Sealing, and cook on manual high pressure for 5 minutes. Turn off the Instant Pot and let the pressure release naturally.

Turn the Instant Pot to Sauté on normal/medium heat. Stir in the cornmeal and cook until the soup is thickened. Serve with garnishes.

Chili-Mac

This dish is somewhere between a soup and a chili. It's simple food that's quick and easy to prepare; kids will love it as much as adults.

=== 6 TO 8 SERVINGS ===

Ingredients

1 teaspoon vegetable oil

1 pound (455 g) ground venison

1 rib celery, thinly sliced

1 small yellow onion, diced

1 green or red bell pepper, diced

1 jalapeño pepper, minced

1 quart (1 liter) beef broth

1 can (16 ounces/455 g) chili beans, undrained

1 can (14½ ounces/411 g) diced tomatoes with onion, undrained

1 to 2 tablespoons chili powder blend, or to taste

¾ cup (90 g) uncooked macaroni

Garnishes: Shredded Cheddar cheese, oyster crackers, sour cream

Directions

Set the Instant Pot to Sauté on normal/medium heat and let it heat up. Add the oil and venison and cook until the venison is no longer pink, stirring frequently to break up the meat. Add the celery, onion, bell pepper, and jalapeño pepper; cook, stirring occasionally, until the vegetables are tender-crisp, about 5 minutes. Turn off the Instant Pot.

Drain off and discard any excess grease. Add the remaining ingredients except the garnishes; stir well. Cover, set the valve to Sealing, and cook on manual high pressure for 5 minutes. Turn off the Instant Pot and let the pressure release naturally. Serve in bowls with garnishes of your choice.

ABOUT CHILE—AND CHILI—POWDERS

"Chile" (with an *e*) refers to hot peppers, which may be whole or cut up, fresh or dried—even smoked. "Chili" (with an *i*) refers to a cooked, stew-like mixture that typically contains meat, peppers, onions, tomatoes, spices, and sometimes—but not always—beans. "Chili powder" (referred to in this book as *chili powder blend*) is a dried mixture of spices that generally includes ground chiles, cumin, salt, paprika, and herbs.

There are many types of chile powders; the most common is ground cayenne, but there are a number of other delicious varieties. Ancho chile powder adds terrific taste, but little heat, to foods. Chipotle powder is made from dried, smoked jalapeños; unlike the ancho powder, chipotle powder packs plenty of heat. If you can't find these chile powders at your supermarket, try a Latin grocery, or order them from Penzeys Spices at www.penzeys.com.

By the way, paprika is another spice made of dried peppers. Spanish paprika is made from special red peppers that are smoked and dried over a hardwood fire; it is available in both sweet and hot varieties (try www.spanishtable.com for some excellent Spanish paprikas). Hungarian paprika is less smoky than Spanish paprika, and also is available in both hot and sweet varieties; Penzeys carries both. Either Spanish or Hungarian paprika has more flavor than the generic paprika sold at most supermarkets.

Steak 'n' Beans Venison Chili

The Instant Pot makes working with dried pinto beans a snap—you can make them in less than an hour from start to finish, with no pre-soaking needed. (See Using Dried Beans on page 126 for more instructions.)

═══════════════ **8 SERVINGS** ═══════════════

Ingredients

½ pound (225 g) dry pinto beans, picked over

1 can (12 ounces/355 ml) beer

3 to 4 tablespoons chili powder blend

2 tablespoons packed brown sugar

½ to 1½ teaspoons Tabasco sauce

1 teaspoon dried oregano leaves

1 teaspoon salt

1½ pounds (680 g) boneless venison steaks or roast, well trimmed before weighing

1 can (28 ounces/794 g) crushed tomatoes, undrained

1 large onion, diced

1 green or red bell pepper, diced

1 rib celery, diced

3 or 4 cloves garlic, minced

Garnishes: Chopped onion, pickled jalapeño slices, shredded cheese, sour cream, crackers

Directions

Soak the beans overnight, or use the Instant Pot method (see sidebar on page 126). When the beans are ready for cooking, drain and rinse in cold water. Set aside.

In the Instant Pot, combine the beer, chili powder, brown sugar, Tabasco, oregano, and salt; mix well. Cut the meat into ⅜-inch (8 mm) cubes; add to the Instant Pot. Pour the tomatoes over the meat. Add ½ cup (120 ml) water to the tomato can and swish it around, then add that water to the pot. Cover, set the valve to Sealing, and cook on manual high pressure for 12 minutes. Turn off the Instant Pot and carefully turn the valve to Venting to release the pressure.

Add the drained beans, onion, bell pepper, celery, and garlic to the Instant Pot. Cover, set the valve to Sealing, and cook on manual high pressure for 8 minutes. Turn off the Instant Pot and let the pressure release naturally. Stir well before serving with the garnishes of your choice.

HOW TO PEEL TOMATOES

Heat a pot of water to boiling. Carefully slip a whole tomato into the boiling water; boil for about 20 seconds, then remove the tomato with a slotted spoon and hold it under cold running water. Cut away the core with a paring knife; the skin should now slip off easily. If I have a lot of tomatoes to skin, I generally do just one or two at a time; it goes quite quickly, and I don't want to accidentally leave tomatoes in the boiling water too long while I'm peeling others.

For most recipes, you'll also want to remove the seeds: Cut the skinned tomato in half across the equator, then turn the tomato cut-side down and gently squeeze to force out the pulpy seed mass (if the tomatoes are not perfectly ripe, you will need to use your fingertips to pull it out). Discard the seeds, skin, and core; cut up the tomato as desired.

Texas Pride Chili (No Beans)

If you can get fresh poblano peppers, substitute two of them for the green bell pepper. This chili has no beans, but kidney beans are served alongside it as a garnish.

5 OR 6 SERVINGS

Ingredients

3 tablespoons olive oil, divided

2 large sweet onions, diced

1 large green bell pepper, diced

4 cloves garlic, chopped

1½ pounds (680 g) boneless venison, cut into 1-inch (2.5 cm) cubes

1 to 2 tablespoons ancho chile powder (see sidebar on page 46)

1 teaspoon chipotle chile powder (see sidebar on page 46)

1 tablespoon ground cumin

¼ teaspoon cinnamon

1 bottle (12 ounces/355 ml) dark beer

1 cup (235 ml) beef broth

1 teaspoon salt

1 can (16 ounces/455 g) kidney beans, drained and rinsed

Garnishes: Pickled jalapeño slices, shredded Cheddar cheese, sour cream, chopped fresh cilantro, diced red onion, diced fresh tomatoes

Directions

Set the Instant Pot to Sauté on normal/medium heat and let it heat up. Add 1 tablespoon of the oil and the onions and cook until just tender. Add the bell pepper and garlic; sauté for about 5 minutes longer. Transfer the mixture to a bowl.

Add another 1 tablespoon of the oil to the Instant Pot and increase the heat to high. Pat the venison cubes dry with paper towels. Add a loose single layer of venison to the Instant Pot and cook until well browned on all sides, turning as needed. Use a slotted spoon to transfer the browned venison to the bowl with the vegetables; brown the remaining venison in the remaining tablespoon of oil.

When the last batch of venison is browned, return the browned meat and the vegetables in the bowl to the Instant Pot, then sprinkle the ancho and chipotle chile powders, cumin, and cinnamon over all; cook for a few minutes, stirring frequently. Pour in the beer, scraping to loosen any browned bits. Cook for 5 minutes, then add the broth and salt. Cover, set the valve to Sealing, and cook on manual high pressure for 20 minutes. Turn off the Instant Pot and let the pressure release naturally. Use a wooden spoon to break up about a third of the meat cubes into shreds; this helps thicken the chili.

Heat the drained kidney beans in a saucepan with a little water (or microwave in a microwave-safe dish until hot). Serve the beans with the other garnishes so each person can add what they choose to their chili.

Venison Stock (Broth)

Choose bones that have some meat still attached; neckbones, backbones, and ribs work particularly well. Browning the bones before adding them to the Instant Pot produces a richer, more flavorful stock, but you can skip this step to save fuss. This stock is unsalted; add salt to taste when you're using the broth in recipes.

6 TO 8 CUPS (1.4 TO 2 LITERS) STOCK

Ingredients

2½ to 3½ pounds (1.1 to 1.6 kg) uncooked venison bones (see note above), cut to fit Instant Pot

1 large onion, quartered

4 carrots, each cut into several chunks

2 ribs celery (including leaves), each cut into several chunks

6 to 8 sprigs fresh parsley

8 whole black peppercorns

2 bay leaves

1 teaspoon vinegar, optional

Directions

Preheat the oven to 450°F (230°C). Place the bones in a roasting pan. Roast, uncovered, until the bones are nicely browned, about 45 minutes.

When the bones are browned, transfer them to the Instant Pot. Pour 1 cup (235 ml) water into the roasting pan; stir to loosen browned bits. Pour the mixture from the roaster into the Instant Pot. Add all the remaining ingredients to the Instant Pot, along with enough water (5 to 7 cups/1.2 to 1.7 liters) to just cover the bones and vegetables; do not fill the pot more than two-thirds full. Cover, set the valve to Sealing, and cook on manual high pressure for 2 hours.

Turn off the Instant Pot and let the pressure release naturally. Use tongs to remove the bones from the Instant Pot. If you want to pick the meat off the bones to use in casseroles or other dishes, set the bones aside to cool; otherwise, discard the bones. Use a ladle to pour the stock into a cheesecloth-lined strainer that has been set over a large pot. Discard the solids in the strainer. Chill the stock, then remove any fat from the surface.

Gamebird Stock (Broth)

When you're boning gamebirds (pheasant, turkey, duck, etc.), save the back and other bones in a resealable plastic bag; keep them in the freezer until you're making a batch of stock, then combine them with wings and drumsticks, which are not as desirable for regular recipes as the more choice parts such as breasts and thighs. This stock is unsalted; add salt to taste when you're using the broth in recipes.

6 TO 8 CUPS (1.4 TO 2 LITERS) STOCK

Ingredients

2 to 3 pounds (1 to 1.5 kg) uncooked gamebird pieces and bones

1 medium onion, quartered

4 carrots, each cut into several chunks

1 rib celery (including leaves), cut into several chunks

6 sprigs fresh parsley

6 whole black peppercorns

1 bay leaf

1 teaspoon dried herb blend

1 teaspoon vinegar, optional

Directions

Combine all the ingredients in the Instant Pot. Add enough water (6 to 8 cups/1.4 to 2 liters) to just cover the bones and vegetables; do not fill the pot more than two-thirds full. Cover, set the valve to Sealing, and cook on manual high pressure for 60 minutes. Turn off the Instant Pot and let the pressure release naturally.

Use tongs to remove the bones from the Instant Pot. If you want to pick the meat off the bones to use in casseroles or other dishes, set the bones aside to cool; otherwise, discard the bones. Use a ladle to pour the stock into a cheesecloth-lined strainer that has been set over a large pot. Discard the solids in the strainer. Chill the stock, then remove any fat from the surface.

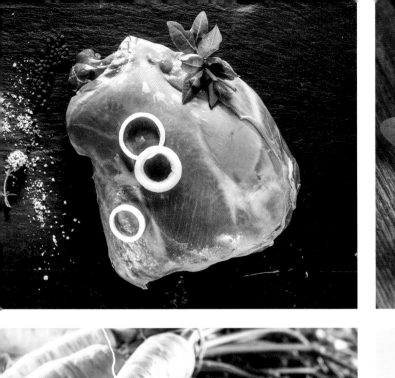

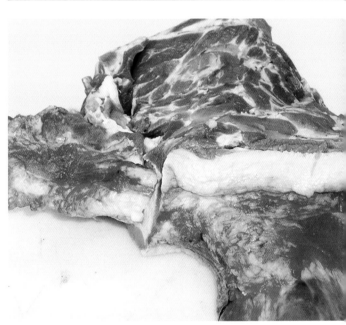

CHAPTER 3

BIG GAME MAIN DISHES

Venison Roast with Root Vegetables and Herbs

This venison pot roast is classic comfort food. The moist heat of the Instant Pot will make the meat tender and delicious.

═══ 6 SERVINGS ═══

Ingredients

2½- to 3-pound (1.1 to 1.4 kg) venison roast

Salt and black pepper

1 tablespoon olive oil

1½ cups (355 ml) red wine

2 tablespoons balsamic vinegar

1 tablespoon dried herb blend

5 carrots, peeled and chopped

4 Yukon gold potatoes, chopped

3 parsnips, peeled and chopped

1 onion, cut into eighths

1 tablespoon cornstarch, stirred into 1 tablespoon water

Chopped parsley

Directions

Season the roast with salt and pepper. Set the Instant Pot to Sauté on more/high heat and let it heat up. Add the oil to the Instant Pot, then add the roast and cook until browned on all sides, about 10 minutes total. Remove the roast from the Instant Pot and set it aside in a bowl.

Pour the wine and vinegar into the Instant Pot and stir to scrape up the browned bits. Stir in the dried herbs, ½ teaspoon salt, and ½ teaspoon pepper, then return the roast and any accumulated juices to the Instant Pot. Cover, set the valve to Sealing, and cook on manual high pressure for 1 hour. Turn off the Instant Pot and let the pressure release naturally.

Add the carrots, potatoes, parsnips, and onion to the Instant Pot, tucking the vegetables around the roast. Cover, set the valve to Sealing, and cook on manual high pressure for 10 minutes. Turn off the Instant Pot and carefully turn the valve to Venting to release the pressure. Using tongs or a slotted spoon, remove the vegetables and roast to a serving platter. Stir the cornstarch mixture into the liquid in the Instant Pot. Turn the Instant Pot to Sauté on more/high heat and cook until the gravy is thickened slightly. Serve the roast and vegetables with the gravy, garnished with parsley.

Venison-Mushroom Stroganoff

This stroganoff is delicious over a bed of soft, wide egg noodles. The sauce will adhere to the noodles for an extra boost of flavor.

5 OR 6 SERVINGS

Ingredients

1½ pounds (680 g) boneless venison round steak

1 tablespoon vegetable oil, plus more as needed

⅓ cup (80 ml) dry sherry

3 sprigs fresh parsley

2 cloves garlic

8 ounces (225 g) fresh mushrooms, sliced

1 cup (140 g) frozen pearl onions, thawed

1 can (10½ ounces/298 g) beef consommé

½ teaspoon dried thyme leaves

½ teaspoon salt

¼ teaspoon pepper

1 cup (227 g) sour cream (reduced-fat works fine)

⅓ cup (45 g) all-purpose flour

Hot cooked noodles or rice

Directions

Cut the venison into 1-inch (2.5 cm) cubes. Set the Instant Pot to Sauté on normal/medium heat and let it heat up. Add the oil and heat until it shimmers. Add half of the venison and brown well on all sides. Transfer the browned venison to a bowl with a slotted spoon. Brown the remaining venison, adding additional oil if necessary; transfer it to the bowl. Add the sherry and ⅓ cup (80 ml) water to the Instant Pot and cook, stirring to scrape up any browned bits, for about a minute. Return the venison to the Instant Pot.

While the venison is browning, chop together the parsley leaves and garlic (discard the parsley stems). Add the parsley mixture, mushrooms, onions, consommé, thyme, salt, and pepper to the Instant Pot; stir well. Cover, set the valve to Sealing, and cook on manual high pressure for 20 minutes. Turn off the Instant Pot and let the pressure release naturally.

At the end of the cooking time, stir together the sour cream and flour in a small mixing bowl. Scoop out about 1 cup (235 ml) of hot liquid from the Instant Pot; stir the liquid into the sour cream mixture and blend well with a fork. Turn the Instant Pot to Sauté on normal/medium heat. Add the sour cream mixture to the Instant Pot. Cook until the sauce thickens and bubbles, stirring once or twice. Serve over noodles or rice.

Three-Bean Casserole with Venison

These tangy, sweet beans, spiked with venison and bacon, will be one of the first things to go at a potluck dinner. Use any type of ground big game that you have on hand—elk, moose, bear, antelope, etc.

8 SERVINGS

Ingredients

6 slices bacon, chopped

1 to 1½ pounds (454 to 680 g) ground venison

1 medium onion, diced

1 can (16 ounces/455 g) baked beans, undrained

1 can (16 ounces/455 g) kidney beans, drained and rinsed

1 can (15½ ounces/439 g) butter beans, drained and rinsed

1 can (8 ounces/227 g) tomato sauce

⅓ cup (73 g) packed brown sugar

2 tablespoons juice from a jar of pickles

1 tablespoon Worcestershire sauce

½ teaspoon prepared mustard

Directions

Set the Instant Pot to Sauté on normal/medium heat and let it heat up. Add the bacon and cook, stirring frequently, until crisp. Use a slotted spoon to transfer the bacon to a plate lined with a paper towel. Drain off all but 1 teaspoon of the drippings from the Instant Pot insert.

Add the venison and onions to the Instant Pot. Cook until the venison is no longer pink, stirring frequently to break up the meat. Drain off and discard any remaining drippings. Add 1 cup (235 ml) water and the remaining ingredients except the bacon to the Instant Pot; stir well. Cover, set the valve to Sealing, and cook on manual high pressure for 5 minutes. Turn off the Instant Pot and let the pressure release naturally. Top with the reserved crumbled bacon just before serving.

Meatballs and Marinara Sauce

Serve the meatballs and sauce with pasta, or use them to make delicious meatball sandwiches according to the variation below.

6 SERVINGS

Ingredients

3 tablespoons olive oil, divided

4 cloves garlic, coarsely chopped

1 can (28 ounces/793 g) whole plum tomatoes, undrained

1 can (28 ounces/793 g) crushed plum tomatoes, undrained

1 teaspoon salt

¼ teaspoon hot red pepper flakes

¼ cup (8 g) chopped fresh basil

1 teaspoon dried oregano leaves

Hot cooked spaghetti or pasta of your choice

For the Meatballs

1 egg

¼ cup (20 g) Italian-seasoned bread crumbs

1 pound (455 g) ground venison

½ pound (225 g) ground pork

¼ cup (30 g) finely grated Parmesan cheese

1 clove garlic, minced

¼ teaspoon salt

Directions

Set the Instant Pot to Sauté on normal/medium heat and let it heat up. Heat 2 tablespoons of the oil. Add the garlic; sauté until the garlic just begins to turn golden. Drain the juice from the can of whole tomatoes and add the juice to the Instant Pot. Cook, stirring frequently, until the liquid cooks away and the sauce thickens, about 5 minutes. Add the whole tomatoes, breaking them up slightly with your hands. Add the crushed tomatoes, salt, and pepper flakes. Cover, set the valve to Sealing, and cook on manual high pressure for 10 minutes. Turn off the Instant Pot and let the pressure release naturally.

Meanwhile, prepare the meatballs: In a large mixing bowl, beat the egg with fork. Stir in the bread crumbs; let stand for 5 minutes. Add the remaining meatball ingredients, mixing well with your hands. Shape the mixture into firmly packed balls that are 1½ inches (4 cm) in diameter. Heat the remaining 1 tablespoon oil in large skillet over medium-high heat. Add the meatballs in a single layer and brown very well on all sides. Transfer the meatballs to the sauce in the Instant Pot; add the basil and oregano and stir gently. Cover, set the valve to Sealing, and cook on manual high pressure for 8 minutes. Turn off the Instant Pot and carefully turn the valve to Venting to release the pressure. Serve the meatballs and sauce over hot cooked spaghetti.

Variation: Meatball Sandwiches

Increase the ground venison to 1¼ pounds (570 g). Prepare the sauce and meatballs as directed above; omit the pasta. Spoon the sauce and meatballs into split French rolls or hoagie rolls, spooning in plenty of sauce. Top each open sandwich with a slice of mozzarella or Provolone cheese (broil open-faced sandwiches until the cheese melts, if you like). Serve with pickled peppers or other condiments of your choice; pour the remaining sauce in a bowl for dipping.

MEATBALL TIPS

- Meatballs are easiest to shape with clean, wet hands, particularly when you're working with a soft meatball mixture such as the Swedish Meatballs (page 63). If your hands become sticky after rolling a few meatballs, rinse them and continue with clean, wet hands.
- Browning meatballs is a little easier in a shallow skillet or sauté pan than in the Instant Pot itself, simply because it's less awkward to turn them with a metal spatula or tongs when you're not reaching into the deep Instant Pot insert.
- Place meatballs in a warm skillet (or Instant Pot, if you wish) as you roll them, distributing them loosely rather than packing them in tightly (if you pack them in too tightly, you won't have room to turn them). As you place each meatball in the skillet, work from one "zone" of the skillet to the opposite edge. By the time you add the meatballs to the last zone, the meatballs that went into the skillet first will probably be ready to turn.
- When a meatball is properly browned, it will release easily from the pan and can be rolled over (rather than picked up and flipped). This is a more gentle method of turning, and works best with delicate meatballs such as the Swedish Meatballs. If the meatball doesn't release with a gentle prod, it isn't ready to turn.

Swedish Meatballs

These meatballs are crowd-pleasers either as a main course or on a buffet table as an appetizer. Serve with cranberry relish, pickled beets, and dill pickles.

4 TO 6 MAIN-DISH SERVINGS, OR 8 TO 10 APPETIZER SERVINGS

Ingredients

½ cup (40 g) bread crumbs

½ cup (40 g) half-and-half

½ teaspoon salt

¼ teaspoon white pepper

⅛ teaspoon nutmeg

2 teaspoons butter

1 small red onion, minced

1 egg

1 pound (455 g) ground venison

½ pound (225 g) ground pork

1 tablespoon honey

1 tablespoon vegetable oil

1 cup (235 ml) chicken broth

1 can (5 ounces/147 ml) evaporated milk

¼ cup (60 g) currant jelly or smooth cranberry sauce

1 tablespoon juice from a jar of pickles

2 tablespoons all-purpose flour, stirred into ¼ cup (60 ml) water

Directions

In a large mixing bowl, stir together the bread crumbs, half-and-half, salt, white pepper, and nutmeg; set aside.

Set the Instant Pot to Sauté on normal/medium heat and let it heat up. Add the butter and the onion and sauté until tender; remove the cooked onion to a large bowl and allow it to cool slightly. Add the egg and bread crumbs and beat with a fork until blended. Add the venison, pork, and honey; mix very well with your hands. Shape into 1-inch (2.5 cm) meatballs (mixture will be very soft; see sidebar on page 62 for tips on making meatballs). Turn the Instant Pot to Sauté on normal/medium heat. Add the oil and half the meatballs, or as many as will fit without crowding; cook until lightly browned on all sides, turning as needed. Use a slotted spoon to transfer the cooked meatballs to a bowl; repeat with the remaining meatballs. Drain off and discard any fat from the Instant Pot insert. With the Instant Pot still set on Sauté, add the broth, stirring to scrape up any browned bits, then stir in the milk, jelly, and pickle juice. Cook for about 5 minutes, stirring frequently. Return the meatballs to the Instant Pot. Cover, set the valve to Sealing, and cook on manual high pressure for 5 minutes. Turn off the Instant Pot and let the pressure release naturally. Gently stir the flour mixture into the sauce. Turn the Instant Pot to Sauté on normal/medium heat and cook until the sauce thickens.

HOW TO MAKE FRESH BREAD CRUMBS

Fresh bread crumbs help provide a more uniform texture in stuffings and meat loaf without absorbing too much of the moisture from the rest of the ingredients. To prepare fresh bread crumbs, use sliced day-old French or Italian bread. Cut the bread into 1-inch (2.5 cm) pieces. Start an empty blender (or food processor fitted with the metal chopping blade). Drop the bread cubes into the running machine through the hole in the top of the blender lid (or through the processor feed tube); chop to a medium-fine consistency. Be sure to keep the lid on as much as possible; the crumbs tend to jump out of the machine during chopping. An average-size slice of bread (3 x 4 x ¾ inch/7.5 x 10 x 2 cm) will make about 1 cup (80 g) of fresh bread crumbs.

Steaks with Wine and Brandy

Serve this elegant dish with roasted or mashed potatoes.

5 OR 6 SERVINGS

Ingredients

½ pound (225 g) thick-sliced bacon

2 pounds (900 g) boneless venison round steaks, ½ inch (1.25 cm) thick, cut into 2- to 3-inch (5 to 7.5 cm) steaks

Salt and pepper

1 large yellow onion, sliced vertically ¼ inch (6 mm) thick

5 carrots, sliced

1 can (14½ ounces/411 g) diced tomatoes, drained

2 cloves garlic, sliced

Leaves from 4 sprigs fresh parsley, chopped

1½ teaspoons crumbled dried rosemary leaves

1½ teaspoons dried thyme leaves

2 bay leaves

2 strips orange zest (orange part only), finely chopped

½ cup (120 ml) brandy

2 cups (475 ml) dry red wine

1 tablespoon Dijon mustard

Directions

Cut the bacon into ½-inch (1.25 cm) pieces. Set the Instant Pot to Sauté on normal/medium heat and let it heat up. Add the bacon and cook until not quite crisp. Use a slotted spoon to transfer the bacon to a bowl; reserve the drippings in the Instant Pot. Sprinkle the venison steaks with salt and pepper and add them to the Instant Pot. Brown in two batches in the reserved bacon drippings. Turn off the Instant Pot. Drain off and discard any excess fat. Add the onion, carrots, tomatoes, garlic, parsley, rosemary, thyme, bay leaves, and orange zest to the Instant Pot.

In a saucepan, heat the brandy over medium heat until just hot. Remove from the heat. Following the information in the sidebar, carefully ignite the brandy and allow it to burn until the flames die completely. Add the wine to the brandy. Cook over medium-high heat until the liquid has reduced to about 1⅓ cups (320 ml); take care, as the wine may ignite during cooking. Stir the mustard into the wine mixture. Pour the hot wine mixture into the Instant Pot. Cover, set the valve to Sealing, and cook on manual high pressure for 30 minutes. Turn off the Instant Pot and let the pressure release naturally. Add the reserved bacon. Discard the bay leaves before serving.

FLAMING LIQUOR

When brandy and other hard liquor is used in cooking, flaming will burn off much of the alcohol, for a smoother, mellower taste. Heat the liquor in a saucepan over low heat until just warm, then remove from the heat. Using a long-handled match, ignite the fumes by holding the lit match at the edge of the saucepan. Here are some safety tips:

- Roll up any long sleeves before starting; tie back long hair.
- Never hold the match in a way that puts your hand over the saucepan (for extra safety, hold the match with tongs when placing it over the saucepan).
- Don't let flames burn underneath a vent hood; grease in the hood filter could ignite.
- Let the flames die completely before adding anything or stirring the contents. Even after the flames have died, watch out for reignition when the pan is moved.

Sweet and Savory Round Steaks

I like to serve this with cooked noodles, but mashed potatoes or rice would also work well. A side dish of broccoli or carrots adds color and nutrition.

─────── **4 SERVINGS** ───────

Ingredients

1½ pounds (680 g) boneless venison, elk, or moose round steaks, about 1 inch (2.5 cm) thick

Salt and pepper

2 tablespoons vegetable oil

⅓ cup (80 ml) beef broth or venison stock (page 51)

Half of a small onion, finely diced

3 tablespoons (36 g) packed brown sugar

¼ cup (60 ml) ketchup

Dried basil leaves

1 tablespoon butter, cut up

Directions

Cut the steak into 8 equal-size pieces. Pound the steak with a meat mallet to ½ inch (1.25 cm) thickness. Sprinkle with salt and pepper. Set the Instant Pot to Sauté on more/high heat and let it heat up. Add the oil, then add steaks (in batches if necessary); brown nicely on both sides, then remove to a plate.

To the Instant Pot, add the broth and 1 cup (235 ml) water and stir to scrape up any browned bits. Return the steaks to the pot and sprinkle the onion, then the brown sugar, evenly over steaks. Distribute the ketchup evenly over the steaks in small dollops. Sprinkle the basil generously over the steaks. Dot with the butter. Cover, set the valve to Sealing, and cook on manual high pressure for 20 minutes. Turn off the Instant Pot and let the pressure release naturally. Serve the steaks with juices from the Instant Pot.

Italian Venison Stew

Serve this delicious stew with buttered noodles, a loaf of bread, and a big green salad.

6 SERVINGS

Ingredients

2-pound (900 g) venison roast, well trimmed before weighing

½ teaspoon salt

½ teaspoon paprika

3 tablespoons olive oil, divided

15 to 20 pearl onions, peeled*

3 cloves garlic, coarsely chopped

1 cup (235 ml) Chianti or other dry red wine

1 can (14½ ounces/411 g) Italian-seasoned stewed tomatoes, undrained

1 can (15 ounces/425 g) garbanzo beans, drained and rinsed

4 ounces (115 g) pitted olives, such as kalamata

8 ounces (225 g) fresh green beans, trimmed and cut into 1½-inch (4 cm) lengths

2 tablespoons all-purpose flour, stirred into ¼ cup (60 ml) water

1 teaspoon dried Italian herb blend

Directions

Rinse the roast and pat it dry. Cut the roast into 1½-inch (4 cm) cubes, trimming away any silverskin (see page 22) or fat. Season with the salt and paprika.

Set the Instant Pot to Sauté on more/high heat and let it heat up. Add half of the oil and heat until it shimmers. Remove half of the venison cubes; add them to the Instant Pot and brown on all sides. Use tongs to transfer the browned venison to a bowl; brown the remaining venison in the remaining oil. Transfer the second batch of browned venison to the bowl.

Add the onions to the Instant Pot; cook until they begin to color, 3 to 5 minutes, stirring several times. Add the garlic; cook for about 1 minute, stirring frequently. Add the wine, stirring to loosen any browned bits. Cook for about 3 minutes, then add the tomatoes with their juices, drained garbanzo beans, and olives; stir to combine.

Return the venison to the Instant Pot. Turn off the Instant Pot, cover, set the valve to Sealing, and cook on manual high pressure for 40 minutes. Turn off the Instant Pot and let the pressure release naturally. Stir the green beans, flour mixture, and dried herbs into the stew, turn the Instant Pot to Sauté on more/high heat, and cook until the green beans are tender.

*To peel pearl onions: Drop them into a pot of rapidly boiling water. Boil for 1 minute, then drain and rinse with cold water. Trim off the root ends; the skins should slip off easily.

Southwestern Venison Stew

I prefer yellow hominy in this stew, but white hominy works fine if that's what you can find. For the beer, I like to use Negra Modelo, a dark Mexican ale.

6 SERVINGS

Ingredients

1½ to 2 pounds (680 to 900 g) boneless venison stew meat

2 tablespoons chili powder blend

1 teaspoon ground cumin

¾ teaspoon garlic salt or plain salt

1 tablespoon vegetable oil

1 medium onion, diced

1 red bell pepper, cut into ¾-inch (2 cm) cubes

1 cup (235 ml) dark beer

2 tablespoons tomato paste

1 tablespoon red wine vinegar

1 can (15½ ounces/439 g) hominy,* drained and rinsed

1 can (4½ ounces/127 g) chopped green chile peppers

1 can (15 ounces/425 g) pinto beans, drained and rinsed

1 tablespoon cornmeal

¼ cup (4 g) chopped fresh cilantro

1 lime, cut into wedges

Directions

Cut the venison into cubes that are approximately 1½ inches (4 cm). Sprinkle with the chili powder blend, cumin, and salt, tossing with your hands to coat evenly. Set the Instant Pot to Sauté on more/high heat and let it heat up. Add the oil and heat until it shimmers. Add half of the venison and brown on all sides; if the oil starts smoking, turn off the Instant Pot and reset to normal/medium heat. Use a slotted spoon to transfer the venison to a bowl. Brown the remaining venison; transfer it to the bowl.

Add the onion and the bell pepper to the Instant Pot; cook for about 5 minutes, stirring frequently. Add the beer to the Instant Pot, stirring to loosen any browned bits, then add the tomato paste and vinegar, stirring to blend. Add the hominy, chiles, beans, and venison to the Instant Pot. Cover, set the valve to Sealing, and cook on manual high pressure for 30 minutes. Turn off the Instant Pot and let the pressure release naturally.

Stir in the cornmeal. Turn the Instant Pot to Sauté on more/high heat and cook until the liquid is thickened slightly. Scatter the cilantro over the stew and serve with lime wedges.

★Hominy, which is also called posole or pozole, is dried corn kernels that have been soaked in a special mixture that swells the kernels; the hull is removed after soaking. Hominy has a pleasantly chewy texture and a rich corn taste. Look for hominy with the canned vegetables.

Sweet and Tangy Asian-Style Venison

Tender venison strips are bathed in a sweet-tangy Asian-influenced sauce . . . perfect with steamed white rice.

4 SERVINGS

Ingredients

1 medium onion, cut in half from top to bottom and sliced

½ cup (120 ml) light soy sauce

1 cup (235 ml) chicken broth

3 tablespoons hoisin sauce*

3 tablespoons packed brown sugar

2 teaspoons minced fresh gingerroot

½ teaspoon hot red pepper flakes

1 pound (455 g) venison roast or steaks, sliced thinly across the grain

¼ cup (60 ml) dry sherry

¼ cup (30 g) cornstarch, mixed with ¼ cup (60 ml) water

4 green onions, sliced (white and green parts)

1 tablespoon sesame seeds

Directions

In the Instant Pot, combine the onion, soy sauce, broth, hoisin sauce, brown sugar, gingerroot, and pepper flakes; stir to blend. Add the venison, pushing the venison into the sauce mixture to coat (do not stir). Sprinkle the sherry over the venison. Cover, set the valve to Sealing, and cook on manual high pressure for 8 minutes. Turn off the Instant Pot and let the pressure release naturally. Add the cornstarch mixture and green onions, turn the Instant Pot to Sauté on more/high heat, and cook until the sauce is thickened. Sprinkle with the sesame seeds just before serving.

Hoisin sauce is a sweet, dark, thick sauce used in Chinese cooking. Look for it in the Asian section of the supermarket, or at a specialty Asian market.

TO BROWN, OR NOT TO BROWN

While you certainly can put roasts, stew meat, and steaks into the Instant Pot with the rest of the ingredients to be pressure cooked without browning the meats on the Sauté setting first, I generally recommend this extra step, which adds both flavor and color to the finished dish and gives the meat a better appearance. After browning the meat, deglaze the pot with some of the liquid used in the recipe; this captures the browned bits that remain behind in the pot and adds depth to the sauce.

Ground meat that's used "loose" in a dish (such as chili, casseroles, or Sloppy Joes) should always be browned before pressure cooking with the remaining ingredients; it's a good idea to brown meatballs as well. Browning ground meat first allows you to drain off and discard any excess fat, which otherwise would be trapped in the dish. It also adds delicious flavor to the finished dish.

Small game and gamebirds can also be browned before the rest of the ingredients are added and pressure cooked, although this is not as important as it is with red meat.

Stuffed Venison Rolls

For a nice twist, add a splash of dry sherry to the beef broth.

6 SERVINGS

Ingredients

1½ pounds (680 g) venison round steak, about ½ inch (1.25 cm) thick

2 slices bacon, diced

¼ cup (40 g) diced onion

2 to 3 ounces (60 to 90 g) fresh mushrooms, sliced

¾ cup (60 g) instant (finely textured) stuffing mix such as Stovetop Stuffing

1½ cups (355 ml) beef broth

1 can (10½ ounces/305 g) condensed cream of mushroom soup

Several lengths of heavy kitchen string

Directions

Cut the steak into 6 equal portions. Pound each steak between sheets of plastic wrap until about ¼ inch (6 mm) thick; set aside.

In a large skillet, cook the bacon over medium heat, stirring frequently, until it begins to crisp. Drain and discard all but about 2 teaspoons of the drippings. Add the onion and mushrooms to the skillet; continue cooking until the vegetables are just tender. Add ½ cup (120 ml) water; heat until just boiling. Remove from the heat; stir in the stuffing mix and set it aside to cool slightly. Divide the stuffing mixture evenly among the pounded steak portions; roll them up and secure with kitchen string.

To the Instant Pot, add the broth. Add the stuffed steaks, nestling them snugly in a single layer; if any stuffing has come out of the rolls or you have a bit left over, distribute it around the edges of the rolls. Cover, set the valve to Sealing, and cook on manual high pressure for 30 minutes. Turn off the Instant Pot and let the pressure release naturally. Use a slotted spoon to remove the rolls to a platter or serving plates. Turn the Instant Pot to Sauté on more/high heat, stir in the condensed soup, and cook to heat through. Serve the venison rolls with sauce from the Instant Pot.

 Variation: Stuffed Venison Rolls with Stuffing on the Side

Pound the venison as directed above; set aside. For the stuffing, use a large skillet to cook 4 slices of diced bacon as directed; drain all but 1 tablespoon of the drippings. Add 1 medium onion, diced, and 8 ounces (225 g) sliced mushrooms to the skillet; cook until tender. Add 1½ cups (350 ml) water to the skillet; heat until just boiling. Remove from the heat; stir in 2½ cups (140 g) of the stuffing mix. Stuff each steak portion with about ¼ cup (30 g) of the cooled stuffing mix; roll and tie as directed. Spoon the remaining stuffing into a greased casserole dish; cover with foil. Continue with the recipe as directed. Place the covered casserole in a preheated 350°F (175°C) oven. Bake for 30 minutes, then remove the foil and bake for 15 minutes longer. Serve the stuffing with the venison rolls and sauce.

Classic Venison Pot Roast

Here's a great way to cook a less-tender venison cut. Browning the meat before cooking produces a rich, flavorful gravy. Serve this with mashed potatoes or sturdy egg noodles.

6 TO 8 SERVINGS

Ingredients

5-pound (2.3 kg) boneless venison chuck roast, tied if necessary

Salt and pepper

1 tablespoon vegetable oil, or more as needed

2 medium onions, coarsely chopped

3 cloves garlic, chopped

1 cup (235 ml) dry red wine

1 can (28 ounces/794 g) plum tomatoes, undrained

3 cups (690 ml) beef broth or venison stock (page 51)

1 tablespoon dried herb blend

4 carrots, cut into 2-inch (5 cm) pieces

2 ribs celery, cut into 2-inch (5 cm) pieces

2 bay leaves

2 tablespoons cornstarch, stirred into ¾ cup (180 ml) water

Directions

Rinse the roast and pat dry with paper towels. Season generously with salt and pepper. Set the Instant Pot to Sauté on more/high heat and let it heat up. Add the oil and heat until it shimmers. Add the roast and brown well on all sides; if the oil starts smoking, turn off the Instant Pot and reset it to normal/medium heat. Transfer the roast to a plate; set aside.

Add the onion and garlic to the Instant Pot (add a bit more oil if necessary) and cook until golden, stirring frequently. Add the wine, stirring to loosen any browned bits. Cook until the wine has reduced by about half. Add the tomatoes and their juices, along with broth and herbs; stir to mix.

Return the roast to the Instant Pot and arrange the carrots, celery, and bay leaves over it. Cover, set the valve to Sealing, and cook on manual high pressure for 90 minutes. Turn off the Instant Pot and let the pressure release naturally.

Transfer the roast, carrots, and celery to a serving platter; discard the bay leaves. Tent the roast loosely with foil. Use a large spoon to skim fat from the surface of the mixture in the Instant Pot. Carefully ladle the mixture from the Instant Pot into a blender or food processor and puree until smooth. Pour the mixture into a saucepan; heat over medium–high heat until just boiling. Add half of the cornstarch mixture to the saucepan and cook, stirring constantly, until bubbly. Add additional cornstarch slurry as needed and continue to cook until the gravy is the desired thickness. Taste for seasoning and adjust if necessary. Serve the gravy with the roast and vegetables.

Simple Sauerbraten

Meat for sauerbraten is usually marinated for several days. This simpler version has the tangy-sweet flavor of sauerbraten—without all the fuss. If you prefer a smooth sauce, pass it through a wire-mesh strainer, pressing on the onions, before serving. (I like the onions with the meat, so I leave them in the sauce even though it is less traditional.)

5 TO 7 SERVINGS

Ingredients

2- to 3-pound (1 to 1.5 kg) venison roast, preferably from the rump or round

Salt and pepper

2 tablespoons vegetable oil

6 whole juniper berries, optional

6 whole cloves

1 bay leaf

2 cups (475 ml) beef broth

⅓ cup (80 ml) red wine vinegar

¼ cup (55 g) packed brown sugar

2 medium onions, sliced, divided

10 gingersnaps (2 inch/5 cm diameter), finely crushed

A small square of cheesecloth and a piece of kitchen string

Directions

Rinse the roast and pat it dry with paper towels. Season generously with salt and pepper. Set the Instant Pot to Sauté on more/high heat and let it heat up. Add the oil and heat it until it shimmers. Add the roast and brown well on all sides; if the oil starts smoking, turn off the Instant Pot and reset it to normal/medium heat. While the roast is browning, tie the juniper berries (if using), cloves, and bay leaf together in a square of cheesecloth; set aside. When the roast is browned, transfer it to a plate.

To the Instant Pot, add the broth, vinegar, and brown sugar, and cook, stirring constantly, until the sugar dissolves and the mixture comes to a boil. Add half of the onions, then the roast, then top with the remaining onions. Tuck in the cheesecloth bag. Cover, set the valve to Sealing, and cook on manual high pressure for 50 minutes. Turn off the Instant Pot and let the pressure release naturally.

Use two forks to transfer the roast to a serving platter. Discard the spice bundle. Set the Instant Pot to Sauté on more/high heat. Stir the gingersnaps into the liquid mixture in the Instant Pot. Cover and cook until the sauce thickens somewhat, about 15 minutes. Slice the roast or break it into large chunks, depending on the cut and tenderness; serve with the sauce (sauce may be strained if you like; see note above).

Savory Boar Roast with Apples

Cooking time depends on the tenderness of the boar roast, as well as the specific cut. This method creates a delicious, dark brown gravy. Serve the roast—and the savory gravy—with mashed white-and-sweet potatoes and a green vegetable.

5 OR 6 SERVINGS

Ingredients

2½- to 3-pound (1.1 to 1.5 kg) wild boar roast, preferably boneless (if using bone-in, choose the larger roast size)

3 cloves garlic, slivered

Salt and pepper

2 tablespoons vegetable oil

1 cup (235 ml) apple juice

3 tablespoons packed brown sugar

1 tablespoon Dijon mustard

2 teaspoons minced fresh gingerroot

¼ teaspoon hot red pepper flakes, optional

1 cup (about 2½ ounces/70 g) dried apple slices

2 tablespoons all-purpose flour, stirred into ¼ cup (60 ml) water

Directions

Rinse the roast and pat it dry with paper towels. With a sharp paring knife, pierce deep slits into the roast; insert a garlic sliver into each slit. Season the roast generously with salt and pepper.

Set the Instant Pot to Sauté on normal/medium heat and let it heat up. Add oil and heat until it shimmers. Add the roast, and brown on all sides.

While the roast is browning, combine the apple juice, brown sugar, mustard, gingerroot, and pepper flakes in a measuring cup or mixing bowl; stir to blend. When the roast is browned, turn off the Instant Pot. Top the roast with the apple slices; pour the apple juice mixture over the roast. Cover, set the valve to Sealing, and cook on manual high pressure for 30 to 45 minutes, depending on the cut (longer for bone-in). Turn off the Instant Pot and let the pressure release naturally. Transfer the roast to a serving platter; let stand for 10 minutes before slicing. Skim the fat from juices in the Instant Pot with a large spoon. Turn the Instant Pot to Sauté on more/high heat, stir the flour mixture into the sauce, and cook until thickened. Serve the roast with the apples and the juices from the Instant Pot.

GETTING DEPTH OF FLAVOR WITH PRESSURE-COOKED DISHES

Roasts and stews cooked in the Instant Pot sometimes seem to be rather one-dimensional. This is partly because the liquid doesn't get as concentrated as it does in many other types of cooking, and also because meat doesn't brown during pressure cooking as it does during oven roasting. One way to add depth of flavor is to brown meats, where appropriate, before adding the remaining ingredients. This extra step takes a bit of extra time, but it adds richness to the finished dish.

For a brighter-tasting dish, consider adding a shower of fresh herbs or a squeeze of citrus juice just before serving.

Venison Roast Braised with Grenadine

I was working with some Persian ingredients and prepared a venison roast with pomegranate syrup. It was delicious: slightly sweet, with an interesting yet easy-to-love flavor. Because pomegranate syrup can be hard to find, I developed this recipe using grenadine syrup, which is similar and much easier to find; look for it at any liquor store, or with the bar mixes in a supermarket.

4 OR 5 SERVINGS

Ingredients

2-pound (1 kg) boneless venison rump roast

Salt and pepper

1 tablespoon olive oil

1 medium yellow onion

½ cup (120 ml) chicken broth

¼ cup (60 ml) grenadine syrup

Directions

Rinse the roast and pat it dry with paper towels. Season the meat generously with salt and pepper. Set the Instant Pot to Sauté on normal/medium heat and let it heat up. Add the oil and heat until it shimmers. Add the roast and brown it well on all sides; if the oil starts smoking, turn off the Instant Pot and reset it to normal/medium heat.

While the roast is browning, cut the onion in half from top to bottom, then cut each half across the equator. Cut each quarter into ¼-inch-wide (6 mm) wedges from top to bottom (rather than half rings). Add the onion wedges to the Instant Pot with the roast, and stir them around occasionally while the roast is browning. In a measuring cup, combine the broth and grenadine.

When the roast is nicely browned, add the broth mixture, stirring to loosen any browned bits. Cook for about 1 minute. Turn off the Instant Pot. Cover, set the valve to Sealing, and cook on manual high pressure for 40 minutes. Turn off the Instant Pot and let the pressure release naturally.

To serve, transfer the roast to a cutting board and let it stand for a few minutes, then cut or break the roast apart into chunks. Place the venison chunks in a serving bowl; pour the juices and onions from the Instant Pot over the top.

Variation: Rabbit Braised with Grenadine

Follow the recipe above, substituting 2½ pounds (1.1 kg) bone-in rabbit pieces for the venison roast. Cook on manual high pressure for 15 minutes, then let the pressure release naturally. To serve, simply pile the cooked pieces in a serving bowl; pour the juices and onion from the Instant Pot over the pieces.

Venison Picadillo

In Cuba, this dish is made with flavorful ground beef chuck. Venison contributes even more flavor and stands up well to the assertive flavors of this traditional dish. Serve picadillo with black beans and rice; for a truly authentic feast, fry up some slices of ripe plantain. Picadillo also makes an outstanding filling for turnovers and other savory pastries.

6 TO 8 SERVINGS

Ingredients

1 tablespoon vegetable oil

2 pounds (910 g) chopped venison (or regular ground venison)

2 medium onions, diced

2 green bell peppers, diced

6 cloves garlic, minced

2 cans (16 ounces/455 g each) whole tomatoes, drained

2 teaspoons paprika

1 teaspoon dried oregano leaves

1 teaspoon ground cumin

1 cup (120 g) chopped pimiento-stuffed Spanish green olives

¼ cup (35 g) chopped raisins

¼ cup (60 ml) red wine vinegar

Directions

Set the Instant Pot to Sauté on normal/medium heat and let it heat up. Add the oil and venison and cook until the meat is no longer pink, stirring frequently to break it up. Add the onions, bell peppers, and garlic; cook, stirring occasionally, until the vegetables are tender-crisp, about 5 minutes. Turn off the Instant Pot. Drain off and discard the excess grease.

Add the tomatoes, crushing them with your hands as you add them to the Instant Pot. Add 1 cup (235 ml) water and the remaining ingredients; stir well. Cover, set the valve to Sealing, and cook on manual high pressure for 5 minutes. Turn off the Instant Pot and let the pressure release naturally.

Barbecue Venison Ribs

For meaty venison ribs, leave a portion of the loin, or an extra outer layer of meat, attached to the ribs when butchering.

=== **4 SERVINGS** ===

Ingredients

4 pounds (1.8 kg) meaty venison ribs, cut apart

1 can (6 ounces/170 g) tomato paste

½ cup (120 g) applesauce

½ cup (120 ml) honey

2 tablespoons cider vinegar

1 tablespoon Worcestershire sauce

1 teaspoon chili powder blend

½ teaspoon Tabasco sauce

½ teaspoon liquid smoke, optional

Half of a medium onion, cut into several chunks

2 cloves garlic

Directions

Heat a large pot of water to boiling. Add the ribs; return to boiling, then reduce the heat and simmer for 5 minutes. Remove the ribs with tongs and pat dry with paper towels. Place the ribs in the Instant Pot.

In a blender, combine the remaining ingredients with ¾ cup (175 ml) water. Blend until the sauce is chunky-smooth. Pour over the ribs in the Instant Pot, turning to coat. Cover, set the valve to Sealing, and cook on manual high pressure for 20 minutes. Turn off the Instant Pot and let the pressure release naturally. Remove the ribs to a serving platter. If the sauce is too liquid, turn the Instant Pot to Sauté on more/high heat, and cook until thickened. Serve the ribs with the sauce.

Honey-Sweet Wild Boar Ribs

Here are fall-off-the-bone-tender boar ribs that have a touch of sweetness to offset the rich boar meat. Cooking time will depend on the age—and tenderness—of the boar; when the ribs are done, the meat will have shrunk away from the bone at the tips and will pull away from the bone easily.

2 OR 3 SERVINGS

Ingredients

1 can (10½ ounces/298 g) beef broth

⅓ cup (80 ml) honey

¼ cup (60 ml) barbecue sauce

¼ cup (60 ml) maple syrup

3 tablespoons Dijon mustard

2 tablespoons soy sauce

Half of a small onion, minced

1 clove garlic, minced

2 to 3 pounds (1 to 1.5 kg) wild boar ribs, excess fat trimmed

Directions

Add the broth, honey, barbecue sauce, syrup, mustard, soy sauce, onion, and garlic to the Instant Pot; stir well. Cut the ribs into 2- or 3-bone portions. Add the rib portions to the sauce in the Instant Pot, turning to coat. Cover, set the valve to Sealing, and cook on manual high pressure for 20 minutes. Turn off the Instant Pot and let the pressure release naturally.

Transfer the ribs to a serving dish. Use a wide, shallow spoon (or a gravy separator) to remove the fat from the juices in the Instant Pot. Turn the Instant Pot to Sauté on more/high heat. Cook the sauce until it reduces by half.

Serve the ribs with the reduced juices (if you like, arrange the ribs on a broiler pan and brush with the reduced juices; broil for a few minutes to heat and crisp the ribs).

CHAPTER 4

SMALL GAME MAIN DISHES

Rabbit and Hominy Stew

Serve this hearty stew with warmed tortillas, diced avocado, shredded cheese, and lime wedges.

Ingredients

1 to 1¼ pounds (454 to 570 g) boneless rabbit meat, cut into bite-size pieces

2 cans (15½ ounces/439 g each) hominy (preferably one yellow and one white), drained and rinsed

1 cup (235 ml) chicken broth

1 can (4½ ounces/127 g) chopped green chiles

1 red bell pepper, diced

1 large onion, diced

3 cloves garlic, minced

1 tablespoon ground cumin

1 tablespoon dried oregano leaves

1 teaspoon paprika

½ teaspoon salt

¼ to ½ teaspoon chipotle powder, optional (see sidebar on page 46)

2 tablespoons cornmeal

¼ cup (4 g) chopped fresh cilantro, optional (but highly recommended)

3 green onions, minced (white and green parts)

Accompaniments: Warmed flour tortillas, diced avocado, lime wedges, shredded cheese

Directions

In the Instant Pot, combine all the ingredients except the cornmeal, cilantro, green onions, and accompaniments; stir well. Cover, set the valve to Sealing, and cook on manual high pressure for 12 minutes. Turn off the Instant Pot and let the pressure release naturally. Stir in the cornmeal. Turn the Instant Pot to Sauté on normal/medium heat and cook until thickened slightly. Stir in the cilantro, if using, and green onions. Serve with the accompaniments of your choice.

Rabbit with Sweet Red Peppers

Cooking rabbit in the Instant Pot is much faster than braising in a Dutch oven, but it will yield similarly succulent, tender meat.

6 SERVINGS

Ingredients

2 wild rabbits, cut into serving pieces

½ teaspoon salt

2 tablespoons olive oil

1 small onion, diced

1 cup (235 ml) chicken broth

2 cloves garlic, thinly sliced

2 tablespoons tomato paste

1 tablespoon drained capers

1 teaspoon paprika

¼ teaspoon white pepper

A pinch of saffron (crumble if using saffron threads)

1 can (14½ ounces/411 g) diced tomatoes, drained

1 jar (12 ounces/340 g) roasted red bell peppers, drained and cut into ½-inch (1.25 cm) strips

2 tablespoons all-purpose flour, stirred into ¼ cup (60 ml) water

Hot cooked rice or noodles

Directions

Pat the rabbit pieces dry with paper towels. Sprinkle the meat with salt; set aside for 5 minutes.

Set the Instant Pot to Sauté on normal/medium heat and let it heat up. Add the oil and heat until it shimmers. Add the onion and the rabbit and cook until golden on all sides.

In a measuring cup, combine the broth, garlic, tomato paste, capers, paprika, white pepper, and saffron; stir to blend. Pour over the rabbit in the Instant Pot. Scatter the drained tomatoes and roasted peppers over the rabbit. Cover, set the valve to Sealing, and cook on manual high pressure for 15 minutes. Turn off the Instant Pot and let the pressure release naturally.

Turn the Instant Pot to Sauté on more/high heat, then stir in the flour mixture and cook until the sauce is thickened slightly. Serve with rice.

 Variation: Upland Gamebirds with Sweet Red Peppers

Substitute 3 partridge, 2 pheasants, or the breast portions from 3 pheasants for the rabbits in the above recipe. Cut the birds into standard cooking pieces: breast halves with or without wings, legs, and thighs (or leg/thigh combinations). Proceed as directed.

Sweet and Sour Rabbit

For a pretty dish, use a mix of red and green bell pepper pieces.

Ingredients

12 to 15 baby carrots, each cut into 2 shorter pieces

1 large green or red bell pepper, cut into large dice

1 small onion, cut into 8 vertical wedges

1½ pounds (675 g) boneless rabbit meat, cut into small bite-size pieces

1 can (8 ounces/227 g) pineapple chunks packed in juice, undrained

⅓ cup (80 ml) seasoned rice vinegar*

¼ cup (55 g) packed brown sugar

2 tablespoons soy sauce

1 tablespoon chopped fresh gingerroot

½ teaspoon hot red pepper flakes, optional

1 clove garlic, pressed or finely minced

2 tablespoons cornstarch, stirred into 2 tablespoons water

Hot cooked rice

Directions

In the Instant Pot, combine the carrots, bell pepper, and onion, stirring to mix. Arrange the rabbit meat on top of the vegetables.

In a mixing bowl, combine the remaining ingredients except the cornstarch mixture and the rice, stirring to blend. Stir in ⅔ cup (165 ml) water. Pour over the rabbit and vegetables. Cover, set the valve to Sealing, and cook on manual high pressure for 12 minutes. Turn off the Instant Pot and let the pressure release naturally.

Stir the cornstarch slurry into the liquid in the Instant Pot. Turn the Instant Pot to Sauté on normal/medium heat and cook until the sauce is thickened slightly. Serve over hot cooked rice.

If you don't have any seasoned rice vinegar, substitute ¼ cup (60 ml) cider vinegar mixed with 2 teaspoons white sugar and 1 tablespoon water.

REMOVING BONES FROM RABBITS

The backstrap (loin) is the largest piece of solid meat on a rabbit, and is easy to bone; simply cut the thick strip of meat away from the backbone and remove any fat. The legs are trickier to bone, and take a bit of time; use a sharp-tipped paring knife and cut as close to the bone as possible. To make it easier to prepare a recipe such as Sweet and Sour Rabbit or Rabbit and Hominy Stew (page 86), separate the rabbit pieces by type when you're packing several for the freezer. Put the boneless backstrap pieces in one package, and the bone-in legs in another. This way you can quickly and easily choose boneless rabbit meat when that's what you need; save the bone-in legs for recipes where the bones don't need to be removed.

Creamy Mushroom Squirrel Bake

Serve this with rice or curly, wide noodles to catch all the sauce.

4 OR 5 SERVINGS

Ingredients

4 slices bacon, diced

8 ounces (225 g) fresh mushrooms, sliced

1 medium onion, diced

1 can (14½ ounces/411 g) beef broth

1 tablespoon lemon juice

2 teaspoons Dijon mustard

2 squirrels, cut into serving pieces

Salt and pepper

1 cup (235 g) sour cream

3 tablespoons all-purpose flour

½ teaspoon dried marjoram or thyme leaves

Paprika

Directions

Set the Instant Pot to Sauté on normal/medium heat and let it heat up. Add the bacon and cook until just crisp, stirring frequently. Add the mushrooms and onion. Cook, stirring frequently, for about 5 minutes. Add the broth, lemon juice, and mustard, stirring to blend.

Pat the squirrel pieces dry. Sprinkle the meat generously with salt and pepper and add the pieces to the Instant Pot. Cover, set the valve to Sealing, and cook on manual high pressure for 15 minutes. Turn off the Instant Pot and the let pressure release naturally.

Spoon out about ⅓ cup (80 ml) of the liquid from the Instant Pot into a bowl. Add the sour cream, flour, and herbs to the bowl with the liquid, stirring to blend well. Add the sour cream mixture to the Instant Pot, stirring to combine. Turn the Instant Pot to Sauté on normal/medium heat and cook until the sauce thickens somewhat; do not let the mixture boil. Sprinkle with paprika before serving.

Squirrel or Rabbit with Mustard

Mustard and blue cheese complement each other very well in this easy dish. Serve with rice, salad, and a vegetable.

5 OR 6 SERVINGS

Ingredients

2 wild rabbits or 3 squirrels, cut into serving pieces

Salt and pepper

2 tablespoons olive oil or vegetable oil

1 medium onion, diced

1 cup (235 ml) chicken broth

½ cup (120 ml) dry white wine

¼ cup (45 g) Dijon mustard

1 teaspoon dried thyme leaves

2 tablespoons all-purpose flour, stirred into ¼ cup (60 ml) water

¼ cup (30 g) blue cheese crumbles

1 tablespoon chopped fresh parsley

Directions

Pat the rabbit or squirrel pieces dry; season generously with salt and pepper. Set the Instant Pot to Sauté on normal/medium heat and let it heat up. Add the oil and heat until it shimmers. Add the game pieces and brown the meat lightly on all sides. Use tongs to transfer the game pieces to a bowl.

Add the onion to the Instant Pot; sauté until just tender-crisp, about 5 minutes. Add the broth, wine, and mustard, and stir to scrape up any browned bits. Return the game pieces to the Instant Pot, and add the thyme. Cover, set the valve to Sealing, and cook on manual high pressure for 15 minutes. Turn off the Instant Pot and let the pressure release naturally.

Stir in the flour mixture. Turn the Instant Pot to Sauté on normal/medium heat and cook until the sauce is thickened slightly. Turn off the Instant Pot, sprinkle in the blue cheese, and let the dish stand until the cheese melts. Sprinkle with parsley before serving.

Country-Style Squirrel Stew

Serve this down-home, simple stew with cornbread and coleslaw.

5 OR 6 SERVINGS

Ingredients

2 large onions, cut into quarters and sliced

2 squirrels, cut into serving pieces

1 teaspoon Worcestershire sauce

½ teaspoon salt

½ teaspoon pepper

1 green or red bell pepper, cut into 1-inch (2.5 cm) cubes

1 pound (455 g) baby carrots

1 pound (455 g) small red or Yukon gold potatoes

1 cup (235 ml) chicken broth

1 tablespoon all-purpose flour, stirred into 3 tablespoons water

Directions

Spread the onions in the bottom of the Instant Pot. Arrange the squirrel pieces on top, tucking them together snugly. Sprinkle the squirrel with the Worcestershire sauce, salt, and pepper. Scatter the bell pepper pieces over the squirrel. Tuck the carrots and potatoes around the outside edges of the pot. Pour in the broth. Cover, set the valve to Sealing, and cook on manual high pressure for 15 minutes. Turn off the Instant Pot and let the pressure release naturally.

Turn the Instant Pot to Sauté on more/high heat and let it heat up. Stir the flour mixture into the liquid in the pot and cook until it thickens slightly.

COOKING TIME AND AGE OF SMALL GAME

Squirrels and rabbits are relatively tender when they're young, but older specimens tend to be tough, requiring longer cooking. Before skinning the game, check for clues as to the relative age.

- Young squirrels have a pointed, tapering tail, while older squirrels tend to have straight tails with blunt ends.
- A young rabbit has soft, flexible ears and a small cleft in the upper lip; ears on an older rabbit are stiff, and the cleft tends to be deeper.
- It's helpful to mark packages of small game as you prepare it for the freezer, noting whether the game is young or mature. If you've thawed some frozen small game that isn't marked, look at the color of the meat. Older animals generally have darker meat than younger animals.

When you're cooking small game in the Instant Pot, check it for tenderness at the time listed by poking it with a fork. If it doesn't yield easily, cover, set the valve to Sealing, and cook on manual high pressure again for a few minutes. Boneless pieces will cook more quickly than bone-in pieces.

Classic Brunswick Stew

This is a two-step recipe. First, the squirrel is stewed until it's tender. The meat is removed from the bone, then the boned meat is combined with hearty vegetables and broth to make a rich stew. You can do the first step one day, then refrigerate the broth and meat for a day or two, until you're ready for the final cooking. Serve this stew with hot buttered biscuits.

6 TO 8 SERVINGS

Ingredients

STEP 1:

3 squirrels

1 quart (1 liter) chicken broth

2 ribs celery, broken into 3 pieces each

1 medium onion, cut into quarters

1 bay leaf

STEP 2:

1 can (14½ ounces/411 g) whole tomatoes, undrained

1 can (10¾ ounces/305 g) condensed cream of celery soup

1 cup (235 ml) hot water

2 medium russet potatoes, peeled and diced

1 medium onion, diced

1 package (9 ounces/255 g) frozen lima beans, thawed

1 cup (165 g) frozen whole-kernel corn, thawed

1 tablespoon packed brown sugar

1 tablespoon Worcestershire sauce

¼ teaspoon freshly ground black pepper

4 or 5 dashes Tabasco sauce

Directions

FOR STEP 1: In the Instant Pot, combine all the ingredients listed in step 1. Cover, set the valve to Sealing, and cook on manual high pressure for 20 minutes. Turn off the Instant Pot and let the pressure release naturally. Remove the squirrel from the broth and set it aside to cool. Strain and reserve the broth; discard the remaining solids.

When the squirrel is cool enough to handle, remove the meat from the bones; discard the bones. At this point, the broth and the squirrel meat can be refrigerated, covered, overnight or for as long as 2 days.

FOR STEP 2: In the Instant Pot, combine the cooked squirrel meat, reserved broth, and all the ingredients listed in step 2. Cover, set the valve to Sealing, and cook on manual high pressure for 4 minutes. Turn off the Instant Pot and carefully turn the valve to Venting to release the pressure.

CHAPTER 5

GAMEBIRD MAIN DISHES

Honey-Mustard Pheasant

The various flavors—honey, mustard, orange, and curry—combine to make a delicious, somewhat sweet sauce. The insides of the orange slices get very soft and taste good, but the peel, while edible, is a bit strong for most people, so you may choose to remove the orange slices before serving. For a milder orange flavor, peel the orange before you slice it; that way, you don't have to worry about removing the orange slices.

4 SERVINGS

Ingredients

1 orange, well washed, sliced (peel before slicing if you prefer; see note above)

1 medium onion, sliced

Bone-in breast halves from 2 pheasants, skin removed (4 pieces total)

Salt

⅓ cup (80 ml) honey

⅓ cup (65 g) prepared mustard

2 tablespoons orange juice

½ teaspoon curry powder blend

2 tablespoons butter, cut up

Directions

Arrange the orange slices evenly in the bottom of the Instant Pot. Top with the onion. Place the pheasant breast halves over the onion; sprinkle with salt to taste. In a small bowl, stir together the honey, mustard, orange juice, and curry powder until smooth. Pour the honey mixture over the pheasant; dot with the butter. Pour ⅔ cup (165 ml) water around the pheasant. Cover, set the valve to Sealing, and cook on manual high pressure for 15 minutes. Turn off the Instant Pot and carefully turn the valve to Venting to release the pressure. Serve the pheasant with the juices from the Instant Pot.

Pheasant Braised with Whole Garlic

This dish contains a whole head of garlic, but don't worry—the garlic becomes mellow and sweet when cooked in this fashion.

4 SERVINGS

Ingredients

Boneless, skinless breast halves from 2 pheasants (4 pieces total)

Seasoned salt

2 tablespoons butter

1 cup (235 ml) chicken broth

½ teaspoon dried marjoram or oregano leaves

¼ teaspoon crumbled dried rosemary leaves

¼ teaspoon sugar

¼ teaspoon salt

A pinch of ground saffron or ground turmeric

1 medium onion

1 small head garlic, loose outer skin removed

1 bay leaf

2 tablespoons all-purpose flour, stirred into ¼ cup (60 ml) water, optional

Directions

Pat the pheasant dry with paper towels. Season generously with seasoned salt. Heat the butter over medium heat in a medium skillet. Add the pheasant; brown lightly on both sides.

While the pheasant is browning, combine the chicken broth, marjoram, rosemary, sugar, salt, and saffron in the Instant Pot; stir to mix. Cut the onion into quarters from top to bottom, then slice each quarter ⅛ inch (3 mm) thick. Add the onion, the whole garlic head, and the bay leaf to the Instant Pot.

When the pheasant has browned, transfer it to the Instant Pot, arranging it on top of the onions. Cover, set the valve to Sealing, and cook on manual high pressure for 12 minutes. Turn off the Instant Pot and carefully turn the valve to Venting to release the pressure. Remove the garlic and allow it to cool enough to handle, then squeeze the cloves back into the dish, discarding the skins. Thicken the juices with the flour mixture if you prefer (see Using Thickeners on page 11) and serve with the pheasant.

HERBS AND SEASONINGS

Some seasonings, such as bay leaves, cinnamon sticks, whole peppercorns, and whole dried peppers, need long simmering to bring out their flavor; these work well in pressure-cooked dishes. (You may want to tie them in a small square of cheesecloth so you can easily remove them from the finished dish.) Dried leafy herbs may lose their punch during pressure cooking; you may wish to taste the sauce just prior to serving and punch it up with a bit more of whatever herb was used. Chopped fresh herbs should be added just before serving; a few minutes' standing time is all it takes to draw out the flavor.

Pheasant and Dumplings

You can substitute partridge, turkey, or grouse for the pheasant in this classic comfort-food recipe. (If you are using wild turkey, increase the pressure-cooking time to 20 minutes.) Plan to serve this dish on a day when you'll have time for a little last-minute prep and final cooking.

4 OR 5 SERVINGS

Ingredients

3 carrots, sliced

1 rib celery, diced

1 small onion, diced

1 teaspoon dried herb blend

1 bay leaf

2 pheasants, cut up and skin removed, or equivalent in pieces (about 3 pounds/1.4 kg)

3 cups (690 ml) chicken broth

1 can (10½ ounces/305 g) condensed reduced-fat cream of chicken soup

1 tube (10 to 12 ounces/289 to 340 g) refrigerated buttermilk biscuits*

Directions

Combine the carrots, celery, onion, herb blend, and bay leaf in the Instant Pot; stir to mix up. Arrange the cut-up pheasant on top, with the legs and thighs on the bottom and the breast portions on top. Pour the broth over the pheasant. Cover, set the valve to Sealing, and cook on manual high pressure for 15 minutes. Turn off the Instant Pot and let the pressure release naturally. With a slotted spoon, transfer the pheasant pieces to a cutting board and set it aside to cool slightly. Use a slotted spoon to pick through the mixture in the Instant Pot to remove any bones. Remove and discard the bay leaf.

Remove the pheasant meat from the bones; discard the bones and any tendons. Tear the pheasant into large bite-size pieces; return the pheasant to the Instant Pot, along with the condensed soup, and stir gently. Turn the Instant Pot to Sauté on normal/medium heat and bring to a simmer. Separate the biscuits and cut each in half if they are large. Arrange the biscuit pieces over the pheasant mixture. With the tempered-glass lid accessory or a regular pot lid that fits (not the sealable Instant Pot lid), cover the pot insert. Cook until the dumplings are cooked through, about 5 minutes; they will no longer look wet on the top and will feel springy when pressed with a fingertip. Serve in soup plates; caution diners to watch for stray bones that may have escaped your notice.

Substitute dumplings made from a buttermilk baking mix if you prefer. Follow the package directions for dumplings on the box of the baking mix. Drop in heaping tablespoons onto the pheasant mix; cook as directed above.

WARNING: *Due to the risk of building dangerous pressure when steaming the dumplings using the Sauté function, do not use the regular Instant Pot lid. Use either a tempered-glass Instant Pot lid (available as an optional accessory) or a regular pot lid that fits on the Instant Pot insert.*

Curried Pheasant or Turkey

Spicy-sweet, with an exotic flavor, this curry is a perfect warmer for winter weather. Be sure to buy unsweetened coconut milk (found with the Asian staples at a supermarket), not the thicker, sweetened coconut cream that is used for tropical drinks.

5 OR 6 SERVINGS

Ingredients

1 pound (455 g) boneless, skinless pheasant or turkey meat, cut into bite-size pieces

1 pound (455 g) orange-fleshed sweet potatoes (about 2 medium), peeled and cut into 1-inch (2.5 cm) chunks

1 green bell pepper, cut into 1-inch (2.5 cm) chunks

1 red bell pepper, cut into 1-inch (2.5 cm) chunks

1 medium Vidalia or other sweet onion, cut into ¾-inch (2 cm) chunks

1 can (14½ ounces/411 g) diced tomatoes, undrained

3 tablespoons peanut butter, crunchy or smooth

1 tablespoon curry powder blend

1 tablespoon minced fresh gingerroot

2 teaspoons minced garlic

½ teaspoon ground cumin

¼ to ½ teaspoon hot red pepper flakes

¾ cup (180 ml) unsweetened coconut milk

2 tablespoons all-purpose flour

For serving: Hot cooked rice, chopped peanuts

Directions

In the Instant Pot, combine the pheasant, sweet potatoes, bell peppers, and onion; stir to mix.

In a small bowl, combine the tomatoes with their juices, peanut butter, curry powder, gingerroot, garlic, cumin, and hot pepper flakes; stir to blend the peanut butter. Pour the mixture into the Instant Pot. Cover, set the valve to Sealing, and cook on manual high pressure for 15 minutes. Turn off the Instant Pot and carefully turn the valve to Venting to release the pressure.

Turn the Instant Pot to Sauté on more/high heat. In a small bowl, combine the coconut milk and flour, stirring to blend. Add to the Instant Pot, stirring well. Cook on high until the sauce thickens somewhat. Serve the curry over hot cooked rice; sprinkle with peanuts.

Small Birds with Sherry and Mushrooms

Serve with rice to soak up all the savory mushroom cream sauce.

3 OR 4 SERVINGS

Ingredients

2 tablespoons butter or margarine

8 to 12 ounces (225 to 340 g) fresh mushrooms (preferably a blend), sliced

6 tablespoons (90 ml) dry sherry

6 to 8 whole quail, woodcock, or doves,* skin removed

Salt-based seasoning blend (such as Montreal seasoning) or plain salt and pepper

⅔ cup (165 g) sour cream

2 tablespoons cornstarch

2 tablespoons grated Parmesan cheese

Directions

Set the Instant Pot to Sauté on more/high heat and let it heat up. Add the butter and let it melt. Add the mushrooms, spreading evenly. Cook without stirring until the mushrooms begin to brown, 3 to 5 minutes. Stir and continue cooking for 3 to 5 minutes longer, until the second side is nicely browned. Add the sherry and ¾ cup (180 ml) water to the Instant Pot. Rinse the birds and pat them dry with paper towels, then sprinkle them generously with your favorite salt-based seasoning blend. Tuck the birds, breast-sides down, into the Instant Pot. Cover, set the valve to Sealing, and cook on manual high pressure for 8 minutes. Turn off the Instant Pot and carefully turn the valve to Venting to release the pressure. Birds should be tender (the flesh on the drumsticks should pull away from the bottoms of the bone). If not, reseal the lid and cook again on high pressure for another 2 minutes. Use tongs and a large slotted spoon to gently transfer the birds to a serving dish; cover to keep warm, and set aside.

In a measuring cup or small bowl, combine the sour cream, cornstarch, and about ¼ cup (60 ml) of the cooking juices, stirring to blend. Stir the sour cream mixture into the Instant Pot. Turn the Instant Pot to Sauté on more/high heat. Cook until the juices have thickened somewhat. Pour the sauce over the birds in the serving dish; sprinkle with the Parmesan cheese. See sidebar on page 107 for a note about small bones.

You could also substitute whole, bone-in breast portions for the whole birds, if that is what you have. Many hunters keep only the breast portions of small gamebirds, and that's a shame, for the legs and thighs of these small birds are delicious and should be savored. Ethics—and good cooking—dictate that the entire bird should be used.

Birds and Biscuits

This down-home dish practically makes itself. While the gravy is thickening at the end, all you need to do is whip up a batch of biscuits (use refrigerated buttermilk biscuits for extra-quick prep) and toss a salad.

═══ **4 SERVINGS** ═══

Ingredients

1 pound (455 g) boneless, skinless upland gamebird meat, cut into ½-inch (1.25 cm) pieces

12 frozen pearl onions, thawed, cut in half

3 carrots, diced

1 jar (2 ounces/57 g) diced pimientos, drained

1 cup (235 ml) chicken broth

½ teaspoon seasoned salt

¾ cup (180 ml) evaporated fat-free milk

1 tablespoon all-purpose flour

1 envelope (generally about 1 ounce/28 g, depending on brand) roasted chicken gravy mix

1 cup (150 g) frozen green peas, thawed (do not substitute canned peas)

Hot biscuits prepared from refrigerated biscuits, boxed buttermilk baking mix, or homemade

Directions

In the Instant Pot, combine the gamebird meat, onions, carrots, pimientos, broth, and salt; stir to mix. Cover, set the valve to Sealing, and cook on manual high pressure for 12 minutes. Turn off the Instant Pot and carefully turn the valve to Venting to release the pressure.

Combine the evaporated milk, flour, and gravy mix in a medium-size mixing bowl; whisk until smooth. Add the milk mixture and peas to the Instant Pot, stirring well. Turn the Instant Pot to Sauté on more/high heat. Cook until the gravy has thickened and the peas are cooked.

While the gravy is thickening, prepare the biscuits. Spoon the bird mixture over the split biscuits.

SMALL BIRDS AND THE INSTANT POT

Pressure cooking tenderizes poultry so much that it may begin to fall apart when you serve it. Bones from larger birds, such as turkey and pheasant, are easy to pick out or nibble around, but those of smaller birds such as quail, dove, and woodcock are harder to deal with. One way to avoid some of the bones is to cut out and discard the backbone before cooking, using kitchen shears.

When eating small gamebirds that have been tenderized in the Instant Pot, watch for the bones, much as you do when eating fish; be sure to tell other diners as well. Don't be too shy to use your fingers to pick up and enjoy every morsel, as though you were eating a tiny fried chicken drumstick. Keep a pretty dish on the table for the discarded bones.

Partridge with Apples and Bacon

Hungarian partridge has more flavor than pheasant and works really well with the flavors of bacon and apple. Chukar partridge are a bit milder than Hungarian partridge, but they are also delicious with this recipe. (I think that sharptail grouse would also be good when prepared in this manner, but I've never had the chance to try it.)

4 TO 6 SERVINGS

Ingredients

2 large McIntosh or Braeburn apples

2 tablespoons orange juice

4 whole Hungarian or chukar partridge, skin removed

1 teaspoon dried marjoram leaves

Seasoned pepper or plain black pepper

8 slices bacon, cut in half crosswise

Directions

Peel, quarter, and core the apples. Cut the apples into slices ½ inch (1.25 cm) thick; distribute them evenly in the Instant Pot. Pour 1 cup (235 ml) water over. Sprinkle with the orange juice.

Cut the partridge into halves (game shears work well for this; simply cut along one side of the breastbone, then up the backbone). Rinse the birds well, paying particular attention to the insides; pat dry with paper towels. Sprinkle with the marjoram, and the pepper to taste. One at a time, place a partridge half in the Instant Pot, topping each half with 2 half slices of bacon. Cover, set the valve to Sealing, and cook on manual high pressure for 15 minutes. Turn off the Instant Pot and let the pressure release naturally. Serve the birds with the cooked apples and juices from the Instant Pot.

Black Bean, Pumpkin, and Gamebird Stew

Be sure to buy a cooking pumpkin for this Mexican-inspired stew—not a jack-o'-lantern! If you can't find a small pumpkin, substitute butternut or another hard squash. Dark meat, such as that from Hungarian partridge or sharptail grouse, is excellent in this stew, but you can use pheasant, turkey, or any other upland gamebird.

4 OR 5 SERVINGS

Ingredients

1 large Vidalia or other sweet onion

1 pound (455 g) boneless, skinless upland gamebird meat, cut into bite-size pieces

1 tablespoon cocoa powder (the kind used for baking)

2 teaspoons dried oregano leaves

1 teaspoon salt

½ teaspoon ground cinnamon

¼ teaspoon white pepper

3 cloves garlic, chopped

Small cooking pumpkin (a 1½-pound/680 g pumpkin is perfect)

1 can (15 ounces/425 g) black beans with cumin, undrained*

¾ cup (180 ml) chicken broth or water

2 teaspoons red wine vinegar

1 tablespoon cornstarch

Hot cooked couscous or rice

Directions

Cut the onion into quarters from top to bottom, then slice each quarter ½ inch (1.25 cm) thick. Scatter the onion in the Instant Pot. In a mixing bowl, combine the gamebird meat, cocoa powder, oregano, salt, cinnamon, pepper, and garlic. Mix well with a wooden spoon, then distribute evenly over the onion.

Peel the pumpkin and remove the pulpy seed mass; weigh out 1 pound (455 g) of the cleaned pumpkin meat (refrigerate any remaining pumpkin for another use). Cut the cleaned, weighed pumpkin into 1-inch (2.5 cm) cubes; distribute evenly over the gamebird meat.

In the same mixing bowl, combine the undrained beans, broth, and vinegar; stir well, then pour evenly over the gamebird meat. Cover, set the valve to Sealing, and cook on manual high pressure for 12 minutes. Turn off the Instant Pot and carefully turn the valve to Venting to release the pressure.

Ladle some of the cooking liquid into a bowl and stir in the cornstarch, then gently stir it back into the mixture in the Instant Pot. If necessary, turn the Instant Pot to Sauté on high and cook until the sauce is slightly thickened. Serve over couscous or rice.

*If you can't find black beans with cumin, use regular black beans with ¼ teaspoon ground cumin added.

Pheasant Legs Cacciatore

When you're packaging pheasants for the freezer, cut them into parts, and package the drumsticks separately. The breasts and thighs can be cooked together in various dishes, but the drumsticks really need longer cooking to become tender. Here's a perfect recipe for them. Keep a pretty dish on the table for the discarded bones.

4 SERVINGS

Ingredients

2 or 3 slices bacon, cut up

8 ounces (225 g) fresh mushrooms, sliced

2 large carrots, coarsely chopped

1 rib celery, coarsely chopped

1 medium onion, coarsely chopped

3 or 4 cloves garlic, minced

½ cup (120 ml) dry white wine

1 can (14½ ounces/411 g) diced tomatoes, undrained

1 tablespoon sugar

1 teaspoon salt

¼ teaspoon hot red pepper flakes

2 bay leaves

12 pheasant drumsticks*

1 teaspoon dried Italian herb blend

2 tablespoons cornstarch, stirred into 2 tablespoons water

For serving: Hot cooked spaghetti, shredded Parmesan cheese

Directions

Set the Instant Pot to Sauté on normal/medium heat and let it heat up. Add the bacon and cook, stirring frequently, until just crisp. Add the mushrooms, carrots, celery, onion, and garlic; cook, stirring occasionally, for 5 minutes longer.

Add the wine; cook for about 5 minutes longer. Add the tomatoes with their juices, sugar, salt, and pepper flakes; stir well. Add the bay leaves. Nestle the drumsticks into the sauce mixture. Cover, set the valve to Sealing, and cook on manual high pressure for 20 minutes. Turn off the Instant Pot and carefully turn the valve to Venting to release the pressure.

Remove and discard the bay leaves; sprinkle the herb blend into the Instant Pot, along with the cornstarch mixture. Turn the Instant Pot to Sauté on more/high heat and cook until the sauce is thickened slightly.

Serve over hot cooked spaghetti, passing the Parmesan cheese separately. Alert diners that there may be a stray bone or tendon that has slipped from a drumstick into the sauce; these pieces are large enough to spot and don't cause a problem, but diners should be made aware of the possibility.

★You can also use a combination of drumsticks and thighs (cut them apart at the joint before cooking); the thigh meat gets tender a bit sooner, but it holds up fine.

Goose-Stuffed Peppers

If you've got a shot-up goose, or some assorted goose parts that you're not sure how to prepare, try this tasty and colorful dish. Be sure to carefully pick out any shot or bone fragments from the meat before chopping it.

4 SERVINGS

Ingredients

¾ pound (340 g) boneless, skinless goose meat

Half of a small onion

1 cup (160 g) cooked rice (brown, white, or wild)

½ cup (50 g) seasoned bread crumbs

1 tablespoon Worcestershire sauce

½ teaspoon salt

1 egg, lightly beaten

4 whole red, green, or yellow bell peppers

2 cans (14½ ounces/411 g each) diced tomatoes, undrained

3 tablespoons packed brown sugar

A few dashes of Tabasco sauce

Directions

Cut the goose meat into 1-inch (2.5 cm) cubes. Chop the meat in a food processor to hamburger consistency; you could also use a meat grinder, running the meat through twice. Transfer the meat to a mixing bowl. Add the onion to the food processor; chop medium-fine, then transfer to the bowl with the meat. Add the rice, bread crumbs, Worcestershire sauce, salt and egg to the mixing bowl. Mix well with a wooden spoon or your hands.

Cut the tops off the peppers. Pull out and discard the core and any seedy ribs without breaking the peppers, which must remain intact. Divide the meat mixture evenly among the peppers, packing it in fairly firmly and mounding the top. Place the peppers upright in the Instant Pot; if they threaten to fall over, prop them up with foil balls.

In the same mixing bowl, stir together the tomatoes and their juices, ½ cup (120 ml) water, the brown sugar, and the Tabasco sauce. Pour the tomato mixture over and around the peppers. Cover, set the valve to Sealing, and cook on manual high pressure for 9 minutes. Turn off the Instant Pot and carefully turn the valve to Venting to release the pressure. Use a meat thermometer to ensure the internal temperature is at least 165°F (74°C); if it's too low, cover and cook at high pressure for another 3 minutes.

If the sauce is too liquid, remove the peppers to serving plates, turn the Instant Pot to Sauté on more/high heat, and cook until the sauce is thickened. Spoon the sauce from the Instant Pot over the peppers when serving.

Variation: Venison-Stuffed Peppers

Follow the directions above, substituting ¾ pound (340 g) ground venison for the goose.

Duck or Goose Cassoulet

Serve this with a green salad and crusty French bread to sop up the juices. If you have some smoked venison sausages, they would be a great choice for this dish.

---
5 OR 6 SERVINGS

Ingredients

4 ounces (113 g) thick-sliced bacon, cut into 1-inch (2.5 cm) pieces

8 ounces (225 g) smoked sausage links, cut into ½-inch (1.25 cm) pieces

1 onion, chopped

5 cloves garlic, thinly sliced

1 cup (235 ml) beef broth

1 can (14½ ounces/411 g) diced tomatoes, undrained

3 tablespoons (45 ml) tomato paste

½ teaspoon salt

1 pound (455 g) boneless, skinless duck (2 mallards) or goose meat, cut into 1-inch (2.5 cm) pieces

2 cans (15 to 19 ounces/425 to 538 g each) cannellini or Great Northern beans, drained and rinsed

1 bay leaf

½ teaspoon dried marjoram leaves

¼ teaspoon dried thyme leaves

¼ teaspoon crumbled dried rosemary leaves

Directions

Set the Instant Pot to Sauté on normal/medium heat and let it heat up. Add the bacon and sausage and cook, stirring frequently, until the bacon is just crisp. When the bacon is done, use a slotted spoon to transfer the bacon and sausage to a bowl. Drain off and discard most of the drippings from the Instant Pot insert. Add the onion and garlic to the Instant Pot; sauté for about 5 minutes.

Add the broth to the Instant Pot, stirring to loosen any browned bits. Add the tomatoes, tomato paste, salt, duck meat, beans, and bay leaf to the Instant Pot. Return the bacon and the sausage to the Instant Pot. Cover, set the valve to Sealing, and cook on manual high pressure for 12 minutes. Turn off the Instant Pot and carefully turn the valve to Venting to release pressure.

Stir in the marjoram, thyme, and rosemary; let stand for a few minutes before serving.

FREEZING TOMATO PASTE

Sometimes, you just need a small amount of tomato paste rather than a full can. Here's what I do with the extra. Line a small baking sheet (or a dinner plate) with waxed paper. Spoon out large dabs of extra tomato paste onto the waxed paper; I make each one a tablespoon because that is a size that is often needed for recipes. Freeze until solid, then roll up the waxed paper and store it in a freezer-weight plastic food storage bag or in a plastic container. When you need a spoonful of tomato paste, just peel a frozen dab off the sheet; it will thaw very quickly.

Duck or Goose and Dressing

Dried apricots give this dish an unexpected touch that goes great with the waterfowl.

=== **6 SERVINGS** ===

Ingredients

1 tablespoon butter or margarine, plus more for the baking pan

2 ribs celery, diced

Half of a medium onion, diced

1 pound (455 g) boneless, skinless duck or goose meat, cut into bite-size pieces

1 package (14 ounces/397 g) herb-seasoned cubed stuffing mix

2 cups (475 ml) chicken broth

4 ounces (115 g) dried apricots, diced

For serving: Prepared gravy

Directions

Butter a deep baking pan that fits in your Instant Pot—a deep 8-inch (20-cm) round cake pan or springform pan will work. Make an aluminum-foil sling (see sidebar, below).

Set the Instant Pot to Sauté on normal/medium heat and let it heat up. Add the butter and let it melt. Add the celery and onion; cook, stirring occasionally, until tender-crisp, about 5 minutes. Add the duck or goose and cook until no longer raw-looking. Turn off the Instant Pot. Add the stuffing mix, broth, and apricots; stir well to mix. Transfer the mixture to the buttered baking pan.

Clean and rinse the Instant Pot insert and return it to the Instant Pot; set a rack inside and pour in 1 cup (235 ml) water. Set the stuffing-filled baking pan on the rack with a sling underneath for lowering and lifting the pan. Cover the Instant Pot, set the valve to Sealing, and cook on manual high pressure for 20 minutes. Turn off the Instant Pot and carefully turn the valve to Venting to release the pressure. If you'd like, crisp up the dressing under the broiler before serving. Meanwhile, prepare the gravy from a packaged mix, or heat gravy from a jar. Serve the dressing with the hot gravy.

USING A FOIL SLING

An 8-inch (20 cm) round baking pan or dish will just fit into a 6-quart (5.5 liter) Instant Pot on top of the rack. To facilitate lowering it into the Instant Pot (and removing it after pressure cooking), make a sling out of aluminum foil: Cut a piece of foil about 20 inches (51 cm) long and fold it lengthwise into thirds to make a long strip. Arrange the strip underneath the baking pan and grasp the ends to lower the pan onto the rack in the Instant Pot. Push the ends of the foil down a bit if necessary to keep them inside the insert. When the dish is ready, use the foil ends to carefully lift the pan up and out of the Instant Pot to a trivet or hot pad nearby.

Shredded Duck Enchiladas

Here's a new way to fix duck that will appeal to anyone who enjoys Mexican-style foods. You may substitute any type of duck, or even goose, for the mallard.

4 SERVINGS (2 PER SERVING)

Ingredients

1 mallard or other wild duck (about 1¾ pounds/800 g), skin removed, cut up

1 envelope (1.25 ounces/35 g) taco seasoning mix

1 medium onion, cut into quarters, then sliced crosswise (so you have quarter-round slices), plus 1 small onion, diced

1 fresh jalapeño pepper

2 or 3 cloves garlic

1⅔ cups (400 ml) tomato juice

8 burrito-size flour tortillas*

1½ cups (170 g) shredded Colby–Monterey Jack cheese blend, divided

Directions

Sprinkle duck pieces with a generous amount of taco seasoning mix and rub it in with your fingertips; set aside. Add the remaining seasoning to the Instant Pot, along with sliced onion. Remove the stem and seeds from the jalapeño pepper (if your skin is sensitive, wear rubber gloves when handling fresh peppers). Chop the pepper and garlic together coarsely; add to Instant Pot. Add the tomato juice to the Instant Pot; stir well, then top with the seasoned duck pieces. Cover, set the valve to Sealing, and cook on manual high pressure for 15 minutes. Turn off the Instant Pot and carefully turn the valve to Venting to release the pressure.

Preheat the oven to 350°F (175°C). Spray a 9 x 9-inch (23 x 23 cm) baking dish with nonstick spray; set aside.

Use a slotted spoon to transfer the duck pieces to a cutting board; cool slightly. Pull the duck meat from the bones; discard the bones and any tendons (watch carefully for small rib bones and shot). Shred the meat with two forks. Divide the meat evenly among the warmed flour tortillas, spooning the meat in a line across the center of each tortilla. Sprinkle the diced onion evenly over the meat. Sprinkle about 1 tablespoon of the cheese over each tortilla. Roll the tortillas up and arrange them in the prepared baking dish. Pour the sauce from the Instant Pot over the tortillas, spreading it evenly. Top with the remaining cheese. Bake until bubbly, about 25 minutes.

★Flour tortillas are easier to roll if they're heated for a minute or so in the microwave, or wrap them in foil and put them in the preheated oven for 5 to 10 minutes.

Variation: Shredded Duck Tacos

Follow the recipe above, but use only 1⅓ cups (315 ml) tomato juice. Eliminate the flour tortillas; you'll need 8 hard (corn) taco shells instead. Reduce the cheese to 1 cup (115 g). After the duck meat is cooked and shredded, return the meat to the sauce. Turn the Instant Pot to Sauté on normal/medium heat and cook until the meat is hot. Serve the meat in hard taco shells, with diced onion, cheese, and any other accompaniments you like (shredded lettuce, pickled jalapeño slices, and sliced or diced avocado work well). This is a saucy taco filling, so the best accompaniments are those that are not too wet.

Orange-Sauced Duck

I like to serve this with hot rice and stir-fried vegetables;
leftovers are great spooned over rice.

4 SERVINGS

Ingredients

1 small orange, well washed

2 whole wild mallards or other medium-size ducks, skin on or removed

Salt and pepper

½ cup (120 ml) orange juice

¼ cup (60 g) port wine or sweet vermouth

¼ cup (60 ml) currant jelly

½ teaspoon dry mustard powder

½ teaspoon chopped fresh tarragon, optional

2 tablespoons cornstarch, stirred into 2 tablespoons water

Directions

Slice the orange and arrange the slices in the bottom of the Instant Pot. Sprinkle the ducks generously inside and out with salt and pepper; arrange on top of orange slices, breast-side up. Pour 1 cup (235 ml) water into the Instant Pot.

In a small saucepan, combine the orange juice, wine, jelly, mustard, and tarragon, if using. Cook over medium heat, stirring constantly, until the sauce bubbles, about 5 minutes. Spoon about half of the sauce over the ducks; stir the cornstarch mixture into the remaining sauce in the saucepan and set aside.

Cover the Instant Pot, set the valve to Sealing, and cook on manual high pressure for 20 minutes. Turn off the Instant Pot and carefully turn the valve to Venting to release pressure. The meat should separate easily from the bone when it is done.

Transfer the ducks to a serving platter. Strain the juices from the Instant Pot into the saucepan with the reserved sauce; discard the orange slices. Heat the sauce over medium heat, stirring frequently, until hot and thickened. Season with more orange juice or jelly if the sauce needs more acidity or sweetness. Season to taste with salt and pepper. Serve the sauce with the ducks.

Variation

This is for those who really love the tangy-sweet flavor of oranges with their duck. Follow the recipe above, adding 1 can (11 ounces/312 g) mandarin oranges, drained, to the sauce during the final heating.

HOW MUCH MEAT WILL I GET FROM A . . .

Some recipes call for a specific amount, by weight, of boneless, skinless gamebird meat. Here's an approximate guide to what you can expect from the birds you're likely to use in this way. All yields are for the specific portion from one bird; for example, "pheasant breast" means the two boneless, skinless breast halves from one pheasant.

SPECIES	YIELD
Pheasant breast	8 ounces/225 g
Pheasant thighs	3½ to 4 ounces/100 to 115 g
Partridge or grouse breast	4 ounces/115 g
Dove breast	1 ounce/30 g
Mallard breast	6 to 8 ounces/170 to 225 g
Small Canada goose breast	12 to 16 ounces/340 to 455 g
Snow or other small goose breast	10 to 11 ounces/285 to 315 g
Giant goose breast	1¼ to 3 pounds/565 g to 1.4 kg
Turkey breast	6½ to 7 pounds/3 to 3.2 kg
Turkey thighs	1 to 1¼ pounds/455 to 565 g

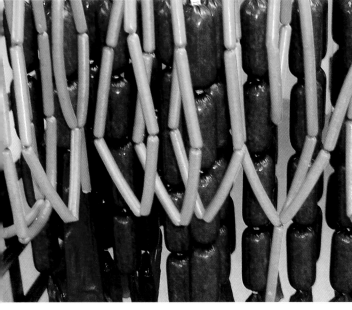

CHAPTER 6

ON THE SIDE

German-Style Potato Salad

Use pepper bacon for extra kick, if you like.

5 OR 6 SERVINGS

Ingredients

¼ pound (115 g) thick-sliced bacon, cut up

1 small white onion, diced

2 ribs celery, diced

2 pounds (900 g) red-skinned potatoes, washed but unpeeled

½ cup (120 ml) cider vinegar or rice vinegar

¼ cup (50 g) sugar

2 tablespoons juice from a jar of pickles

1 teaspoon salt

1 teaspoon dry mustard powder

½ teaspoon celery seed

1 tablespoon cornstarch, stirred into 1 tablespoon water

Optional garnishes: Sliced hard-cooked eggs, sliced radishes, chopped fresh parsley

Directions

Set the Instant Pot to Sauté on normal/medium heat and let it heat up. Add the bacon and cook until just crisp, stirring frequently. Drain and discard all but about 1 tablespoon of the drippings from the Instant Pot insert. Add the onion and celery to the Instant Pot; cook until tender-crisp, stirring occasionally. Turn off the Instant Pot.

Slice the potatoes about ¼ inch (6 mm) thick; place them in the Instant Pot. Combine the vinegar, ½ cup (120 ml) water, sugar, pickle juice, salt, mustard powder, and celery seed in a measuring cup or bowl; stir well to dissolve the sugar, then add to the Instant Pot and stir gently with a wooden spoon to combine. Cover, set the valve to Sealing, and cook on manual high pressure for 3 minutes. Turn off the Instant Pot and carefully turn the valve to Venting to release the pressure.

Turn the Instant Pot to Sauté on normal/medium heat and gently stir in the cornstarch mixture; cook until it thickens slightly. Take the insert out of the base and set aside to cool somewhat. Garnish the potatoes with the sliced eggs and radishes; sprinkle with chopped parsley. Serve warm.

Baked Beans with Smoked Sausage

*These baked beans are fairly sweet; reduce the molasses a bit
if you prefer beans that are less sweet.*

8 TO 10 SERVINGS

Ingredients

1 pound (455 g) dry navy beans, picked over

1 medium onion, chopped

1 can (8 ounces/227g) tomato sauce

¾ cup (180 ml) molasses

¼ cup (55 g) packed brown sugar

1 tablespoon Worcestershire sauce

1½ teaspoons dry mustard powder

¼ teaspoon pepper

¾ pound (340 g) smoked, fully cooked venison sausage, diced

Directions

Soak the beans overnight, or use the Instant Pot method (see sidebar). Drain and rinse in cold water. Put the drained beans in the Instant Pot. Add the onion, tomato sauce, molasses, brown sugar, Worcestershire sauce, mustard powder, and pepper; stir well. Add enough water to cover the beans by 1 inch (2.5 cm). Cover, set the valve to Sealing, and cook on manual high pressure for 8 minutes. Turn off the Instant Pot and let the pressure release naturally. If the bean mixture is too thin, remove about 1 cup (235 ml) of beans and mash with a potato masher; return the mashed beans to the pot, stirring in well. Turn the Instant Pot to Sauté on normal/medium heat. Add the sausage and cook until the sausage is heated through.

USING DRY BEANS

Dry beans are best when soaked before cooking. Rinse and pick over the beans, tossing any stones or other foreign material you may find. Here are two methods for soaking, the traditional long soak overnight and a quick Instant Pot method.

- The overnight method: Put the beans in a container, add cold water to cover by at least 2 inches (5 cm), and simply let the beans soak on the countertop overnight. Drain and rinse the beans; they are now ready to use in a recipe.
- The Instant Pot method: Put the beans in the Instant Pot and add water to cover by 1 inch (2.5 cm). Cover, turn the valve to Sealing, and cook on manual high pressure for 5 minutes. Turn off the Instant Pot and let the pressure release naturally. Drain and rinse the beans; they are now ready to use in a recipe.

Dry beans are best when they are fresh; older beans that have been lying around the store shelf or in your cupboard for a year or more may never become tender. Buy beans from a store that has a good turnover (rather than from a convenience store, for example, where beans may sit on the shelf for a long time).

Easy Rice Pilaf

This sweet and nutty pilaf is easy to put together a few hours before dinner. It goes particularly well with a simple venison roast, or with roast duck, goose, pheasant, or turkey.

6 SERVINGS

Ingredients

Half of a small onion, diced

1 rib celery, diced

¼ cup (20 g) diced dried apple slices

¼ cup (25 g) diced dried apricots

1 box (7 ounces/198 g) white-and-wild-rice blend*

1 tablespoon butter or margarine, cut into pieces

¼ cup (26 g) coarsely chopped pecans or walnuts

Directions

In the Instant Pot, combine the onion, celery, apple, apricots, and rice blend (including seasoning). Add the butter and 2 cups (475 ml) water; stir to combine. Cover, set the valve to Sealing, and cook on manual high pressure for 20 minutes. Turn off the Instant Pot and let the pressure release naturally. Fluff the rice and fold in the pecans.

I like Zatarain's (New Orleans Style) Long Grain & Wild Rice. If you're using a different type, you may need to adjust the amount of water used. Note that this technique is not intended for use with "quick-cook" rice blends.

Variation: Easy Rice Pilaf with Sausage

For a more substantial dish, cook ¼ pound (115 g) breakfast-style sausage (pork or venison) in a skillet over medium heat until no longer pink, stirring to break up the meat. Drain; add the sausage to the Instant Pot with the rice and other ingredients, and proceed as directed.

Easy Acorn Squash

Here's an easy side dish that comes out tender and tasty. Feel free to use any type of seasoned salt or pepper that you like in place of the plain salt and pepper.

===== **2 SERVINGS** =====

Ingredients

1 acorn squash (about 1¼ pounds/570 g)

2 tablespoons butter or margarine, divided

1 tablespoon packed brown sugar, divided

3 tablespoons dried cranberries, divided

Salt and pepper

Directions

Add 1½ cups (355 ml) water to the Instant Pot and fit a rack in the bottom of the insert. Break off the stem from the squash if necessary. Using a large knife, carefully cut the squash in half from top to bottom (it's easiest to do this with the squash lying on its side on the cutting board; cut between the natural ribs, taking care so the knife doesn't slip). Scoop out and discard the seeds and strings. Place the squash halves cut-side up on the rack in the Instant Pot. Divide the butter evenly between the two halves, following with the sugar and dried cranberries. Sprinkle the squash generously with salt and pepper. Cover, set the valve to Sealing, and cook on manual high pressure for 5 minutes. Turn off the Instant Pot and let the pressure release naturally. To serve, use two large spoons to remove each squash half from the Instant Pot, taking care not to collapse the shell. Serve the squash in the shell, or scoop out into a serving dish if you prefer.

Variation: Savory Stuffed Acorn Squash

In a medium skillet over medium heat, brown 4 ounces (115 g) uncooked venison sausage (casings removed if links) until the meat loses its pink color. Add half of a small onion, chopped, and cook until the onion is tender-crisp. Remove the sausage from the heat. Stir in the dried cranberries. Divide the filling mixture evenly between the squash halves. Top the filling evenly with the brown sugar. Sprinkle with salt and pepper. Cook as directed.

Late-Summer Succotash

Succotash comes to us from the early Native Americans; its name derives from the Narragansett word msíckquatash, *which translates to "boiled whole-kernel corn." There are many versions of succotash today; this one uses fresh corn for an extra-sweet flavor.*

6 SERVINGS

Ingredients

4 whole ears fresh corn on the cob

1 cup (235 ml) chicken broth

1 package (9 ounces/255 g) frozen lima beans, thawed

1 red bell pepper, cut into ½-inch (1.25 cm) cubes

Half of a small onion, diced

2 cloves garlic, minced

1 bay leaf

½ teaspoon dried marjoram leaves

¼ teaspoon salt

A few grindings of black pepper

Half of a 10¾ ounce (305 g) can condensed cream of celery soup (reduced-fat works fine)

Chopped fresh parsley

Directions

Cut the kernels off the corncobs; add the kernels and any corn milk from the cutting board to the Instant Pot. Hold each cut cob over the Instant Pot and use a table knife to scrape the milky juices into the pot; discard the cobs as each is scraped.

Add the remaining ingredients except the condensed soup and parsley to the Instant Pot; stir to mix well. Cover, set the valve to Sealing, and cook on manual high pressure for 4 minutes. Turn off the Instant Pot and carefully turn the valve to Venting to release the pressure. Discard the bay leaf. Stir in the condensed soup and sprinkle the succotash with fresh parsley.

Instant Pot Dressing

When the oven is bursting at the seams during holiday time, prepare this delicious dressing in the Instant Pot.

=== **8 TO 10 SERVINGS** ===

Ingredients

8 ounces (225 g) uncooked venison sausage (casings removed if links)

3 ribs celery, sliced

1 medium onion, diced

1 cup (235 ml) chicken broth

1 teaspoon dried herb blend

¼ cup (55 g) butter or margarine, plus more for pan

6 cups (215 g) dry cubed bread (see sidebar)

½ cup (50 g) coarsely chopped pecans

1 small apple (peeled or not, as you prefer), diced

Directions

Butter a deep baking pan that fits in your Instant Pot—a deep 8-inch (20 cm) round cake pan or springform pan will work. Make an aluminum-foil sling (see sidebar, page 115).

In a large skillet, cook the sausage over medium heat, stirring frequently to break it up, until some of the fat is rendered. Add the celery and onion and continue to cook, stirring frequently, until the meat is no longer pink and the vegetables are tender-crisp, about 5 minutes. Remove from the heat; drain and discard the excess grease. Add the broth and herb blend to the skillet, stirring to mix. Set aside.

Set the Instant Pot to Sauté on normal/medium heat and let it heat up. Add the butter and let it melt. Add the bread cubes and cook until golden brown, stirring frequently. Turn off the Instant Pot. Add the pecans, apple, and sausage mixture from the skillet to the bread cubes in the Instant Pot; stir well to combine. Transfer the mixture to the prepared baking pan.

Clean and rinse the Instant Pot insert and return it to the Instant Pot; set a rack inside and pour in 1 cup (235 ml) water. Set the stuffing-filled baking pan on the rack, with the sling underneath for lowering and lifting the pan. Cover the Instant Pot, set the vent to Sealing, and cook on manual high pressure for 20 minutes. Turn off the Instant Pot and carefully turn the valve to Venting to release the pressure. If you'd like, crisp up the dressing under the broiler before serving.

> ### MAKING BREAD CUBES FOR DRESSING
>
> When you're preparing recipes that call for cubed dry bread, you could use prepackaged unseasoned stuffing cubes, but it's best to make your own bread cubes. Cut a denser bread, like French or Italian bread, into ¾- to 1-inch (2 to 2.5 cm) cubes. Spread them out on a baking sheet and let them dry overnight, stirring several times if possible. If you're in a hurry, spread the cubes out in a single layer on a baking sheet, and bake in a 300°F (150°C) oven until dry and crisp, about 20 minutes.

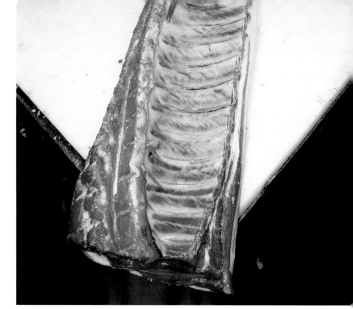

CHAPTER 7

PARTY TIME

Party Nachos with Venison

Nachos are always a crowd pleaser. Try this delicious variation at your next gathering.

Ingredients

1 can (15 ounces/425 g) chili beans, undrained

2 pounds (900 g) venison steaks

1 envelope (1.25 ounces/35 g) taco seasoning mix

1 can (14½ ounces/411 g) diced tomatoes, drained

For serving: Tortilla chips, shredded Monterey Jack cheese, sour cream, salsa, sliced pickled jalapeño peppers, diced tomatoes, diced onions, shredded lettuce

Directions

Spread the undrained beans in the Instant Pot. Top with the steaks; sprinkle the taco seasoning evenly over the meat. Top with the tomatoes and 1 cup (235 ml) water. Cover, set the valve to Sealing, and cook on manual high pressure for 30 minutes. Turn off the Instant Pot and let the pressure release naturally.

Transfer the meat to a cutting board; cool slightly. While the meat is cooling, use a potato masher to mash the beans in the Instant Pot. Use two forks to shred the meat apart on the cutting board; discard any bones or tough material. Return the shredded meat to the Instant Pot; stir well. Turn the Instant Pot to Keep Warm.

To serve, each guest places some tortilla chips on a plate, then tops the chips with a scoop of the meat mixture and adds toppings as desired. The meat mixture can sit in the Instant Pot on Keep Warm for up to 2 hours (stir occasionally).

Variation: Duck or Goose Nachos

Substitute 2 pounds (900 g) boneless, skinless goose or duck (or 2½ to 3 pounds/1.1 to 1.4 kg bone-in thighs) for the venison steaks. Proceed as directed; cooking time may be slightly less.

Manhattan-Style Wild Boar or Javelina Chunks

This adults-only appetizer uses the basic ingredients of a Manhattan cocktail, combined with wild boar or javelina, for an unusual party dish.

6 TO 8 APPETIZER SERVINGS

Ingredients

2 pounds (900 g) boneless wild boar or javelina chops, well trimmed before weighing

Salt

2 tablespoons butter, divided

1 tablespoon vegetable oil

¾ cup (180 ml) bourbon or blended whiskey

6 tablespoons (90 ml) sweet vermouth

2 teaspoons sugar

4 generous dashes Angostura bitters (from liquor store or in the bar-mix area of a supermarket)

15 maraschino cherries, stems removed, halved

1 tablespoon juice from the maraschino cherries

1 tablespoon cornstarch, stirred into 1 tablespoon water

Directions

Cut the boar into 1-inch (2.5 cm) cubes; salt generously. Set the Instant Pot to Sauté on more/high heat and let it heat up. Add half of the butter and all of the oil and let the butter melt. Add half of the boar chunks; brown on all sides. Use tongs to transfer the boar to a bowl. Add the remaining butter to the Instant Pot and brown the remaining boar chunks. Transfer the boar to the bowl.

Add the bourbon, vermouth, sugar, and bitters to the Instant Pot, stirring to loosen any browned bits. Cook for about 5 minutes. Return the boar chunks to the Instant Pot and add ½ cup (120 ml) water, the cherries, and cherry juice. Cover, set the valve to Sealing, and cook on manual high pressure for 30 minutes. Turn off the Instant Pot and let the pressure release naturally. Turn the Instant Pot to Sauté on normal/medium heat. Stir in the cornstarch mixture and cook until the sauce thickens. Turn the Instant Pot to Keep Warm to serve at a party.

Venison Sausage Pizza Dip

Offer a basket of breadsticks, pita wedges, or bread chunks to accompany this spicy dip.

Ingredients

1 pound (455 g) uncooked venison sausage (remove casings if links)

1 small onion, minced

Half of a green or red bell pepper, diced

1 jar (26 ounces/737 g) marinara or other prepared pasta sauce

2 teaspoons dried Italian herb blend (or a mix of oregano and basil)

¼ teaspoon hot red pepper flakes, or to taste

1 can (4¼ ounces/120 g) chopped black olives, drained

¼ cup (30 g) shredded Parmesan cheese

Directions

Set the Instant Pot to Sauté on normal/medium heat and let it heat up. Add the sausage and cook, stirring frequently to break up the meat, until some of the fat is rendered. Add the onion and the bell pepper and continue to cook, stirring frequently, until the meat is no longer pink and the vegetables are tender-crisp, about 5 minutes. Turn off the Instant Pot. Drain off and discard any excess grease.

Add ½ cup (120 ml) water and stir to loosen any browned bits. Add the pasta sauce, herbs, and pepper flakes; stir well. Cover, set the valve to Sealing, and cook on manual high pressure for 5 minutes. Turn off the Instant Pot and let the pressure release naturally.

Stir in the olives and Parmesan cheese. Turn the Instant Pot to Keep Warm to serve at a party. If the dip gets too thick after a while, stir in a bit of hot water.

Sweet and Sour Meatballs

For this crowd-pleasing party appetizer, roll the meatballs small and serve with a jar of cocktail forks next to the Instant Pot.

8 TO 10 APPETIZER SERVINGS*

Ingredients

1 egg

2 tablespoons all-purpose flour

½ teaspoon salt

1½ pounds (680 g) ground venison

Half of a small onion, grated or finely minced

1 to 2 tablespoons vegetable oil, as needed

1½ cups (350 ml) pineapple juice

¼ cup (60 ml) rice vinegar or cider vinegar

¼ cup (55 g) packed brown sugar

2 tablespoons soy sauce

2 tablespoons ketchup

1 teaspoon minced fresh gingerroot

3 tablespoons cornstarch

1 green or red bell pepper (or a mix), cut into ½ x 1½-inch (1.25 x 4 cm) strips

4 ounces (110 g) fresh snow pea pods, cut in half crosswise

Directions

In a mixing bowl, blend together the egg, flour, and salt with a fork. Add the venison and onion; mix gently but thoroughly with your hands. Shape the mixture into 1-inch (2.5 cm) meatballs. Set the Instant Pot to Sauté on normal/medium heat and let it heat up. Add 1 tablespoon of the oil and heat until it shimmers. Add the meatballs in a single layer and brown on all sides; you may need to brown in two batches. Add the remaining oil if needed. Transfer the browned meatballs to a plate. Turn off the Instant Pot.

Pour the pineapple juice into the Instant Pot, stirring to scrape up any browned bits, then add the vinegar, brown sugar, soy sauce, ketchup, and gingerroot; mix well. Return the meatballs to the Instant Pot. Cover, turn the valve to Sealing, and cook on manual high pressure for 5 minutes. Turn off the Instant Pot and let the pressure release naturally.

Spoon a little of the sauce into a small bowl and stir in the cornstarch. Gently stir the cornstarch mixture back into the meatballs, along with the bell pepper strips and the pea pods. Turn the Instant Pot to Sauté on normal/medium heat and cook until the vegetables are just tender and the sauce is thickened. Turn the Instant Pot to Keep Warm to serve at a party.

You can also make larger, walnut-size meatballs to serve as a main dish for 4 to 6 people. They're great with hot white rice and canned chow mein noodles.

 ### Variation: Sweet and Sour Meatballs with Goose or Duck

Follow the recipe above, except you'll be chopping your own goose or duck to replace the venison. You'll need 1 pound (454 g) boneless, skinless goose or duck and ½ pound (225 g) boneless pork chops with a bit of fat. Cut the waterfowl and pork into 1-inch (2.5 cm) cubes, then chop to hamburger consistency. Proceed as directed above.

Mulled Cranberry-Apple Cider

This delectable beverage serves two purposes: It provides a delicious warmer for a fall or winter party, and it makes your kitchen smell great.

12 SERVINGS

Ingredients

1 quart (1 liter) processed apple cider (not the refrigerated kind)

1 quart (1 liter) cranberry juice cocktail

1 cup (235 ml) brandy, optional

1 orange, well washed, thinly sliced

2 whole cinnamon sticks

4 slices peeled fresh gingerroot, each about ¼ inch (6 mm) thick

10 whole cloves

½ cup (120 ml) honey

Directions

Combine all the ingredients in the Instant Pot. Cover, set the valve to Sealing, and cook on manual high pressure for 1 minute. Turn off the Instant Pot and carefully turn the valve to Venting to release the pressure (if you are using brandy, make sure there are no open flames nearby, as steam released from the valve will contain evaporated alcohol). The mulled cider can be kept on the Keep Warm setting for several hours. Serve hot.

Hot Spiced Wine

Start a batch of this in advance of a party, and turn the Instant Pot to Keep Warm so it's hot and ready when guests arrive. You might want to offer a plate of orange and lemon slices so guests can float one in their cup.

=== **8 TO 10 SERVINGS** ===

Ingredients

3 tea bags

½ cup (100 g) sugar

1 bottle (750 ml) cabernet sauvignon or other dry, medium-bodied red wine

1 cup (235 ml) dark rum

1 can (6 ounces/177 ml) frozen orange juice concentrate, thawed

3 whole cloves

1 stick cinnamon

Directions

In a saucepan or teakettle, bring 2 cups (475 ml) water to a boil. Remove from the heat; immediately add the tea bags and steep the tea for 5 to 10 minutes. Remove and discard the tea bags. Add the sugar to the tea; stir until the sugar dissolves. Add the sweetened tea and the remaining ingredients to the Instant Pot, stirring to blend. Cover, set the valve to Sealing, and cook on manual high pressure for 1 minute. Turn off the Instant Pot and carefully turn the valve to Venting to release the pressure (make sure there are no open flames nearby, as the steam released from the valve will contain evaporated alcohol). The spiced wine can be kept on the Keep Warm setting for several hours. Serve hot.

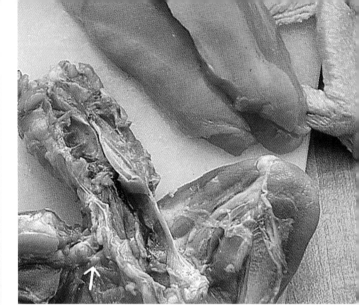

APPENDICES

PANTRY LIST

Dry beans, grains, and pastas

cornmeal

couscous

egg noodles

lentils

macaroni

pearled barley

pinto beans

rices: white and brown

spaghetti

thin rice sticks

wild rice and white-and-wild-rice blend

Canned broths and soups

beef broth

beef consommé

chicken broth

condensed beef broth

condensed cream of celery soup

condensed cream of chicken soup

condensed cream of mushroom soup

condensed cream of potato soup

Canned beans

baked beans

black beans with cumin

butter beans

cannellini or Great Northern beans

chili beans

garbanzo beans

kidney beans

pinto beans

Canned tomatoes

crushed tomatoes

diced tomatoes

diced tomatoes with onion

marinara or other pasta sauce

stewed tomatoes

tomato juice

tomato paste

tomato sauce

whole plum tomatoes

Canned vegetables and fruit

capers

green chile peppers, chopped

hominy

mushrooms, sliced

olives: chopped black, pitted kalamata,
    and pimiento-stuffed Spanish green

pimientos, diced

pineapple chunks

potatoes, whole

roasted red bell peppers

Spices and dried herbs

ancho chile powder

ancho chiles, whole

bay leaves

black peppercorns

cayenne pepper, ground

celery seed

chili powder blend

chipotle chile powder

cinnamon, ground
cinnamon sticks
cloves, whole
cumin, ground
curry powder blend
dried herb blends
dry mustard powder
garlic salt
hot red pepper flakes
juniper berries
marjoram
nutmeg
oregano
poultry seasoning
rosemary
saffron
seasoned pepper, salt-based seasoning blend
taco seasoning mix
thyme
turmeric, ground
white pepper

Alcohols and mixers
Angostura bitters
beer
bourbon
brandy
dark rum
dry sherry
grenadine
port
red wine
sweet vermouth
white wine

Dried fruits and nuts
apple slices
apricots
dried cranberries
pecans or walnuts
raisins

Other
all-purpose flour
cornstarch
dry onion soup mix
evaporated milk
fish sauce
liquid smoke
roasted chicken gravy mix
soy sauce
sweeteners: honey, maple syrup, molasses,
    brown sugar
turkey gravy mix
unsweetened coconut milk
vinegars: red wine, rice, balsamic, cider

PRESSURE COOKING AT HIGH ALTITUDES

The boiling point of water is lower at higher altitudes, so you'll have to cook your Instant Pot dishes slightly longer if you're working more than about 2,000 feet (610 m) above sea level.

AT OR ABOVE	INCREASE TIME BY	TO CALCULATE, MULTIPLY TIME BY	EXAMPLES
2,000 feet (610 m)	5%	1.05	increase 20 to 21 min
3,000 feet (915 m)	10%	1.1	increase 20 to 22 min
4,000 feet (1220 m)	15%	1.15	increase 20 to 23 min
5,000 feet (1524 m)	20%	1.2	increase 20 to 24 min

ADAPTING STOVETOP AND SLOW-COOKER RECIPES FOR THE INSTANT POT

Many of your favorite recipes for dishes cooked on the stovetop or in a slow cooker are easily adaptable to last-minute cooking in the Instant Pot. Braises, soups, beans, pot roasts, and of course long-cooked stews are ideal candidates. A few rules of thumb to keep in mind:

- Tougher cuts of meat—those that would require low-and-slow cooking in moist heat on the stovetop or in a slow cooker—are best for pressure cooking.
- If the recipe doesn't already include a total of at least 1 cup (235 ml) of runny liquid (water, broth, or similar), add more to make up the difference. Remember that the steam from the liquid is what allows the Instant Pot to build up pressure. You can cook off excess liquid or thicken the sauce after pressure cooking, if necessary.

- Add any thickening agents, like a cornstarch or flour slurry (see page 11), at the end of the process, after the pressure-cooking step has been completed.
- Add condensed soups or dairy products after the pressure-cooking step has been completed. Thick condensed soups can clog up the Instant Pot and prevent pressure from building. Dairy products can curdle and separate under high-heat conditions—don't let the dish boil after adding them.
- Check the cooking time tables in the instruction manual that came with your Instant Pot, or the approximate cooking times for game meats on page 14, and use those times as a starting point. If there are vegetables in the dish that might become overcooked in the time it takes to cook the meat or other long-cooking ingredients, pressure cook your dish in two stages.

INDEX